LADY
IN
RED

Where is Your Head?

LADY
IN
RED

Where is Your Head?

... Surviving a
Brain Injury
And
Coma

by **Carolann deBellis**

ARPress
ILLUMINATING IDEAS,
EMPOWERING VOICES

ARPress
45 Dan Road Suite 5
Canton, MA 02021

Hotline: 1(888) 821-0229
Fax: 1(508) 545-7580

Ordering Information:
Quantity sales. Special discounts are available on quantity purchases by corporations,associations, and others. For details, contact the publisher at the address above.

Printed in the United States of America.

ISBN-13:   Softcover   979-8-89330-020-8
                     eBook   979-8-89330-021-5

Library of Congress Control Number: 2024900578

CONTENTS

FOREWORD

I met Carolann in the summertime of 1967 as a junior high student living in Connecticut. She and her cousin Michael were from Philadelphia and were visiting their cousin in our Connecticut upper class neighborhood. We became friends instantly and enjoyed many summers together, she visiting Connecticut and me visiting Philadelphia during summer break. It was a blissful time—Carolann was always so much fun. As the years drifted on, I moved to California and we lost contact.

My understanding is that Carolann became a hairdresser, like her father, in a prestigious salon in Center City. She made phenomenal money and was able to travel while being married to her best friend for twelve years. She enjoyed her many friends and family and they enjoyed her bubbly personality and infectious spirit.

Fast forward to 2006. Because of the internet, Carolann and I were reconnected. I learned of her accident and that she was writing a book to help others who suffered brain injuries or knew someone who had suffered a brain injury. She needed help to get her book typed and ready for a publisher. I felt as if God was asking me to be that person, and invited Carolann to California.

So, after 30 years, Carolann and I were reunited! She made two trips to California, once in April 2007 and then again in January of 2008, and put the finishing touches on her many years of note-taking. It has been my joy and absolute privilege to be a small part of

Carolann's journey in putting her experience in print. My hope is that many people will benefit from reading her incredible story!

~Meg Henninger Roberts

HEAD INJURY

THE SILENT EPIDEMIC

Head injuries take the lives of more people under the age of 44 than any other single cause—more than spinal cord injuries and all neurologic diseases except stroke. Males 16 to 24 years of age are most affected.

Each year, *one million* persons incur traumatic brain injuries. Most such injuries result from automobile accidents, with falls and gunshot wounds the other major factors. About 100,000 of these individuals die of their head injuries. And of the survivors, about 200,000 experience physical or psychological deficits so severe that they cannot resume their former lifestyle.

With improved immediate response and more sophisticated emergency treatment, more persons now survive head injuries. But their needs have become more and more complex.

The rehabilitation process for individuals with head injury involves an array of services and programs not usually required with other disabilities. Even minor head injuries can produce psycho-social and cognitive deficits ranging from maladjustment to partial or total functional disability.

Help—for head-injury survivors, their families and the healthcare professionals who treat them—begins with information. With a support group. With a referral to specialized providers of care. And for the population at large, help begins with educational programs and legislative initiatives designed to prevent further head injuries and to ease their human and financial toll.

The National Head Injury Foundation and its Pennsylvania affiliate, the Keystone State Head Injury Foundation, are leaders in this nationwide effort. We coordinate state and local activities on behalf of persons with head injury. Our purpose is simply stated: together, we seek the best quality of life for head-injury survivors and their families. We invite you to join us in pursuit of our goal.

Reprinted from the Keystone State Head Injury Foundation

I would like to acknowledge that 5% of the proceeds of this book will go to The National Head Injury Foundation at

333 Turnpike Rd.
Southboro, Mass. 01772
(619) 485-9950

and 5% will go to the Magee Rehabilitation Hospital at

6 Frankin Plaza
Philadelphia, PA 19102
(215) 587-3000

because without them, people with brain injuries and physical disabilities would NEVER make it in our world today.

DEDICATION

—Thank you God.
You knew I needed to come back to
give and definitely learn more.

I am dedicating this book to Michael Biello

You have been in my life since the day I was born. I always
loved the closeness we had with each other growing
up. Michael, you are one of the reasons I am still here.
Without your <u>meaningful</u> and <u>spiritual</u> help every single
day while I was in my coma and after I was in and out of
consciousness, I wouldn't be here today writing this book.

Much, much love to you, cousin.
Thank you with all my heart and soul.

ACKNOWLEDGEMENTS

I would love to express my love and gratitude to the following people:

Tommy, Hon, Sweet Face, my BEST FRIEND for twelve years and husband for eight years, thanks for helping me understand everything that happened to me before I woke up one month later aware that I had been injured. You stood by my side the whole time I was in the hospital and rehab. The girl you were in love with was not there anymore. I know you lost a lot . . . Your Love, your business, your life as you knew it. I'll never forget all that you've done and how much you really loved me. For that I will always love you and never forget you.

Thank you again Tommy

Ida Ray, Aunt Ida Auntie who helped me <u>more than she'll ever know.</u> It was like me having a second chance at being raised again. From 34 years old to about 44-45 years old. In that frame of time it was like I was a little girl to a teenager. Then I became an adult. After you taught me from teenager to adult . . . . as you taught me when I spent summers with you in Dallas and Avon from 9 to 14 yrs. old. You were ALWAYS like a second mother to me ;)

Thank you Aunt Ida for being there for me and teaching me again!
I love you, Auntie.

Thanks to <u>all</u> of my dear family members, aunts uncles, cousins for being there for me . . . and teaching me again! Especially my mom—Anna DeBellis, my dad—Rudolph DeBellis, my sister—Renee Sisto, my sister—Janice DiBerardino and my brother Rudy DeBellis. They all know what they did. You all did many <u>good things</u> to help me <u>learn again!</u>

I love you guys.

Renee, also thanks for making me realize what the name of my book should be.

. . . . Renee was coming home from seeing me in a coma and heard the song "Lady in Red" by Chris DeBurgh on the car radio. She had to pull over, she was crying SO HARD. Red is my color; everyone close to me knows. The words that really hit her were . . . . "I've never seen you look so lovely as you did tonight, I've never seen you shine so bright . . . It's where I want to be . . . But I hardly know this beauty by my side, ILL NEVER FORGET THE WAY YOU LOOK TONIGHT. The lady in red . . . I love you"

. . . They said I looked like an angel as I was laying there in a coma.

I love you, sister.

Janice, thanks for trying to type my book . . . very hard to understand my writing.

I love you, sister.

Maureen Matticoli, cousin Maureen, thanks for typing Michael's journal for me. And thanks for not being busy every time I had a question about this book.

I love you, cuz.

Michael Biello, cousin Michael, thank you for helping me put this book together in the right way. And for all the times you helped me put my personal life together in the right way.

I love you, cuz.

Dan Martin, Danny, thank you for being by Michael's side through all his emotions with me . . . Boy were there emotions, I hear.

I love you, Danny.

Richard Damien, Michael's inspiring spiritual teacher & healer . . . you told Michael "not to worry. Your cousin is on the other side, she's coming back. She's going to write a book to help others. I see her on Oprah Winfrey." . . . . You also HELPED ME others. I see her on Oprah Winfrey." . . . . You also HELPED ME WHEN I DID COME BACK.

Thank you Richard
YOUR FABULOUS!

Joan Pileggi, Joanie, Mommy, my boss at "Pileggi on the Square," eight years of doing hair there.

Thank you for giving me the opportunity to try again . You took me back to work after only four months out of rehab. You knew I wasn't the old Carol anymore. Being a hairstylist, I had to be <u>social</u> and <u>graceful</u> and <u>tolerant</u> to clients. I wasn't the sweet, cheerful Carol I used to be, even though I could still cut hair. You also taught me how to be professional and to always say the right thing <u>prior</u> to my accident. I always loved you.

Thanks Mommy

Thanks to my friends who still remained my friends . . .

Denise Nanni-Campo, who has been my friend since first grade—52 years. Thank you for understanding my craziness after my brain injury and for remaining my friend. You'd say, "Carolann, you're the same, you just regressed . . . you are like a teenager now! You have to learn again," you said. Denise is the longest, truest, real friend I have.

I love you, girlfriend.

Celeste-Spata-Jackson, whom I've known for 46 years, your friendship has stayed the same! For example, you sent me a card as I was going through difficult times.

"Dear Carol" it read, "I'm your friend and I'm here if you NEED ME. I can see you are struggling right now. Things that were once familiar to you have changed, leaving you to feel a little lost and worried. Life challenges us to grow by putting us in different situations. But if things seem too difficult, remember that I'm your friend, and you mean a lot to me. I'm here if you need me."

Love,
Celeste
Thanks, I love you, girlfriend.

Michele Morroney, whom I've known for 45 years, also remained my friend. You took me with "a grain of salt." When I told you how people would say that I'm so different, you'd say "Don't they know you got hurt? It's not your fault! You'll be fine, don't listen or let them get you down, Carol."

Thanks, Michele, I love you.

My married friend Andrew, thank you for giving me the desire to see the next day of my life! You came into my life when I needed a man the most! You gave me <u>so much</u> attention and liked me so much. I know I would have at least tried to take my life at that horrible, traumatic time I was in, instead of just thinking about it!

Thanks Andrew—I hope God understands!

Gennaro Charles Durante, Jerry, sweetheart, sweets ☺ . . . you taught me that "SEX IS NOT LOVE." You helped me deal with and feel okay not having a man next to me every minute like I needed in the past. You also made me feel MORE FEMININE than I ever have in my life. Thanks for giving me my INDEPENDENCE.

Boy do I love and like you. ☺

Meg Henninger-Roberts, thank you for coming back into my life after 30 years ☺ . Without you, this book would never have been typed. I never knew there was a computer that typed as you spoke into it ☺ Alleluia! It's like we saw each other only yesterday. And let me not forget her loving husband, Jim, whose patience was magnificent in teaching Meg and me how to use his computer.

Thanks, guys. I love you.

Valerie Beltran, thank you for taking time out of your busy college schedule to type this book for me. After I deleted by accident all Jim helped me to do on his computer, I really needed you! You typed this entire book in less than a week. No one believes in my words more than you do. Your tears while typing are a testament to the impact of this project. It is fate that brought us together.

Thank you so, so much

Alexander M. Mackie, Sandy, thank you for being the editor of my book. Through your busy schedule, you helped me so much . . . . More than you know.

Thank you so much

Dorothea Christopher, Thea, thank you for re-typing my book after it was edited. And getting my cover in color and red dress to be sent to publisher . . . . Through your busy life.

Thank you, Thea

Janice DiBernardino, Jan my loving, helpful sister . . . "AFTER ALL THAT WAS SAID AND DONE" you helped me put my book together AGAIN. With things I forgot and wording it the right way, when it needed to be . . . . FINALLY getting it ready for the publisher ☺ I love you sister

. . . Quotations in this book that do not have "who quoted" is because I do not know who they are. I either heard someone say it or read it somewhere and I didn't remember who wrote it. Many quotes move me, and I write them down . . . my refrigerator is filled with quotes. ☺

. . . Some of this book is a little crude. I said the "F" word many times when I got sad and mad after my brain injury.

. . . Also forgive me if I repeat myself . . . my memory is bad and I sometimes forget I already said it. ☹

FACTUAL—MEDICAL SUMMARY

CAROLANN DEBELLIS—DELCOLLE

May 29, 1989

Carol Ann DelColle is a married woman, high school graduate, presently 34 years of age (DOB: 4/17/53) who was injured on 1/19/87 when the automobile in which she was a passenger was involved in a collision on the New Jersey Turnpike.

On 1-19-87, plaintiff was a passenger in a vehicle being operated by Rudolph DeBellis which was traveling from Philadelphia to New York City via the New Jersey Turnpike. There were five people in the car. Plaintiff was seated in the left rear and her sister, Janice DeBellis, was seated in the middle rear.

It was raining when the vehicle left Philadelphia. When the vehicle got to Elizabeth, NJ on the New Jersey Turnpike, the roads became icy. At this point, the northbound portion of the New Jersey Turnpike consists of six lanes, two sets of three lanes each divided by a median. The DeBellis vehicle (a front wheel drive automobile) was traveling in the outer set of the northbound lanes (the lanes closest to the right side shoulder) and was driving in the left lane of that set. The vehicle was traveling at approximately 35-45 miles per hour. Mr. DeBellis attempted to move into the middle northbound operating lane when the vehicle's rear wheels lost traction and the vehicle started to slide from side to side. He tried to stop the sliding motion by pumping the brakes and steering into the skid. The front of the vehicle skidded into the left hand medial barrier and bounced back. The vehicle came to a complete stop at a right angle to northbound traffic with its front end facing the medial barrier. As the vehicle was sitting there in a stopped position, it was struck broadside on the left side by the defendant's vehicle. It is important to note that Mr. DeBellis' vehicle had been in a stopped position for at least a few seconds prior to being struck by the defendant's vehicle. See police report for accident diagram.

Following the accident, it took approximately 45 minutes to extract plaintiff from the vehicle. She was unconscious at the scene of the accident and was brought by ambulance to Newark, NJ. She was admitted through the Emergency Room to the Surgical/Intensive Care Unit for closed-head trauma, cerebral concussion, fractures fo the right acetabulum (hip bone) and symphysis pubis (fibrocartilaginous union of pubic bone), and a right clavicular fracture (collarbone). She remained in a coma for approximately ten (10) days. A CT scan of her brain revealed diffuse cerebral edema and her stay in the S.I.C.U. was complicated by a urinary tract infection. There was also an episode of influenza while in the N.I.C.U. She also required a cardiac consultation due to some EKG changes. On February 6, 1987, plaintiff was transferred to a floor with private duty nursing services provided by Kimberly Services, Inc. She received private nursing care until she was discharged.

Plaintiff needed private duty nurses to monitor the effect of her medications, dispense her medications, maintain her IV infusions, observe and assess her changing conditions, monitor her respiratory status, maintain her nutritional status and skin integrity, assess her electrolyte imbalance, prevent contractures and muscle atrophy and maintain a safe environment to ensure Plaintiff's safety. She wore a brace for three weeks for the clavicular fracture. She was treated for cerebral edema and with bed rest for her lower extremity fracture. Her primary treating physicians during this hospitalization were Kevin C. Aurori, M.D. and Dr. Fred Lax. She received the following medications while at University Hospital: Ampicillin (I mg. IV every

6 hours)Zantac (150 mg. twice daily), Dilantin (150 mg. every 6 hours), Theragram (5 cc. daily), Feosol (375 mg. Three times daily), Maalox (30 cc. every 4 hours) and continuous IV at 40 cc. per hour of Dextros and half saline with potassium chloride added.

On February 12, 1987, plaintiff was transferred by ambulance from University Hospital to Magee Rehabilitation Hospital in Philadelphia. Her attending physician was Lawrence J. Horn, M.D. Her Magee admission diagnosis was double hemiparesis (muscle weakness on one side of the body)and cognitive deficits secondary to closed-head injury with bifrontal hygromas (cystic cavities filled with lymph), status post right clavicular fracture and status post pelvic and possible right hip fractures. Her physical examination revealed that neurologically she was quite lethargic. She followed commands but was not entirely cooperative because of her easy fatigueability and distractiblility. She showed impaired attention and deficits in terms of calculation skills. Cranial nerves revealed a possible left field cut neglect.

While at Magee, beginning on March 10, 1987, and ending on March 23, 1987, plaintiff was administered the following tests by Brenda M. Ivker, Ph.D., a psychologist: Halstead-Reitan Neuropsychological Test Battery, Wechsler Memory Scale, Rey Auditory-Verbal Learning Test and Peabody Picture Vocabulary Test. The tests revealed that plaintiff was functioning overall at the bottom of the low-average range with stronger verbal than visuospatial abilities, that she was relatively strong in tasks which reflected her previous verbal ability and relatively weak on visuomotor tasks and tasks which require current attention, concentration, learning and memory, and that she had difficulty on tasks which require mental flexibility and problem solving. Her medications were changed from Dilantin to Tegretol (1200mg. daily). These medications were prescribed to prevent seizures.

Plaintiff remained an in-patient at Magee Rehabilitation Hospital through March 26, 1987. Upon her discharge, it was noted that plaintiff continued to demonstrate impairments in terms of her memory, time and repetition of mental processing. She also lacked insight into her problem areas as she continued to deny having any significant cognitive problems. Her discharge medication was Tegretol, 200 mg. daily to prevent seizures.

Upon her discharge from Magee, plaintiff was seen in Out-patient therapy at the Out-patient Brain Injury Follow-up Clinic. It was noted that following her discharge plaintiff still required assistance in initiating activities and encouragement to engage in laundry activities, cooking, and general home care. She continued to have impairment in terms of memory, time and repetition of mental processing. It was also noted that plaintiff was at risk for seizures and that she continued to lack insight into cognitive deficits associated with traumatic head injury. Furthermore, it was felt that her difficulty in initiating activities would eventually interfere with vocational goals. Her last brain injury follow-up evaluation revealed that she continues to suffer from memory changes, impulsivity and social inappropriateness. She continues to treat with Out-patient Therapy at the Out-patient Brain Injury Follow-up Clinic.

Plaintiff complained of blurred vision towards the left and was referred to Wills Eye Hospital where she was seen by Dr. Thomas Bosley on April 14, 1987. His diagnosis was that plaintiff had a mild dyschromatopsia (partial color blindness) on the left, a mild afferent (carrying toward) pupillary defect on the left side, and incomplete, non-congruous left homonymous hemianopia (loss of vision affecting inner half of one and outer half of the other visual field) and a mild midrasis on the left with mild ptosis (drooping of upper eyelid) on that side. It was Dr. Bosley's diagnosis that plaintiff has a partial right optic tract syndrome which is the cause of her visual problems to the left. Her vision to the left has not improved and she continues to treat with Dr. Bosley. Furthermore, her driver's license is in the process of being revoked due to her loss of peripheral vision in the left eye.

In November, 1987, she saw her nutritionist, Dr. Allan Magaziner, complaining that she was extremely tired, her short term memory had decreased, she had become increasingly impatient and her menstrual cycle had become irregular. Dr. Magaziner prescribed Synthroid for plaintiff.

On May 9 and 10, 1988, plaintiff was reevaluated at Magee. She was administered the following tests: Halstead-Reitan Neuropsychological Test Battery, Wechsler Memory Scale, Rey Auditory Verbal Learning Test, Peabody Picture Vocabulary Test, Benton's Judgement of Lines Orientation Test and Minnesota Multiphasic Personality Inventory. These test revealed that plaintiff's abilities had not significantly improved since the previous testing in March 1987. Plaintiff was functioning overall at the bottom of the average range while visual-spatial abilities were in the low average range. She was weak on tasks which require analysis of contours and eye-hand coordination. Dr. Ivker felt that this was impacting upon plaintiff's hairdressing skills and that she was being taxed beyond her ability. Overall, plaintiff demonstrated learning and memory difficulties in all spheres tested.

At the end of June 1988, Plaintiff commenced a 30 week program of cognitive therapy at Magee Rehabilitation Hospital. This therapy consists of reading, writing and spelling classes, psychological counseling and group therapy. She attended classes four days per week. Plaintiff continues to treat with Dr. Horn and Brenda Ivker, psychologist, at Magee Rehabilitation Hospital, approximately every six months. She continues to suffer from loss of peripheral vision on her left side which will affect the status of her driver's license.

Plaintiff also continues to suffer from the following problems:

Impaired balance
Impaired coordination
Lack of concentration
Impaired visual analysis
Impaired hand-eye coordination
Impaired short-term memory

Impaired fine motor skills
Standing intolerance
Easy fatigueability
Constant dull pain in cervical and thoracic areas
Impaired concentration
Impaired sense of smell
Impaired ability to follow sequential instructions
Impaired tolerance level
Impaired ability to perform household chores
Impaired ability to prepare for daily activities
Frustration at inability to recover
Mood swings
Resentment and confusion regarding marital obligations
Insecurity in marital relationship
Loss of interest in having children
Strained relationships with family members
Sense of detachment

To date, plaintiff's medical expenses are as follows:

University Hospital, Newark, NJ	
(In-Patient 1/19-2/12/87)	$35,685.30
Dr. Kevin Aurori	1,080.00
Faculty Practice Service	3,910.00
Kimberly Nurses	3,681.01
Medi-Call Ambulance Service	438.00
Magee Rehabilitation Hospital	36,203.68
(In-Patient 2/12-3/26/87)	
Wolfson and Marlowe Associates	75.00
Franklin Town Rehab. Assoc.	3,465.00
Neuro-Ophthalmologic Assoc.	600.00
Dr. Don Koepsell	60.00
Dr. Daniel Bowerman	28.00
Dr. Allan Magaziner	236.00
Dr. Leslie Rose (Endocrinologist)	120.00
Total To Date	$85,581.99

Plaintiff has received $10,000.00 in no-fault medical benefits from her own automobile insurance carrier. Plaintiff has unreimbursed medical expenses of $75,581.99 to date. Plaintiff's medical expenses are ongoing.

At the time of the accident, plaintiff was employed by Pileggi On The Square as a commission hair stylist. Her weekly salary is computed upon a percentage of her gross sales. Her annual earnings are as follows:

1987-$ 9,532.00 (year of accident)
1986-$24,146.00
1985-$26,124.00
1984-$19,518.50

As a result of the accident plaintiff was out of work from the date of the accident through 5/15/87. She returned to work part time until 12/31/87. She finally resigned on 7/30/88 because her accident related symptoms prevented her from adequately performing her duties.

Plaintiff's 1987 tax return declares income of $9,532.00. Her average earnings for the years 1985-86 amount to $25,135.00. Her wage loss for the year 1987, based solely upon her two previous years earnings, is at least in the sum of $15,603.00. Plaintiff's wage loss is continuing.

Plaintiff has received $5,000.00 in no-fault wage loss benefits from her own automobile insurance carrier.

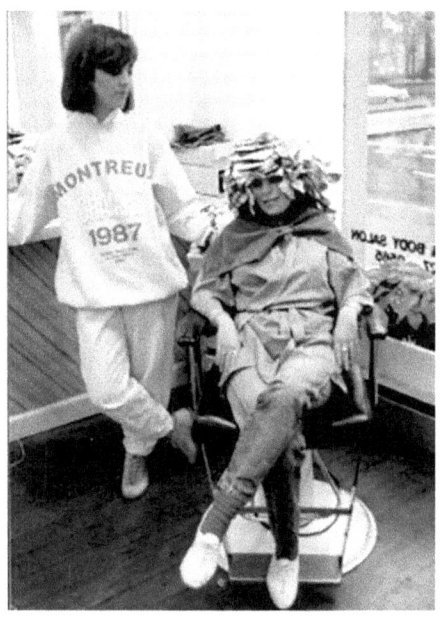

Day before accident doing hair at *Pileggi On The Square* . . .
Wore same outfit . . . They had to cut it off my body ☹

This song is where I got the name of my book. As my sister was driving home from seeing me in a coma the song played and she had to pull over because she was crying. Besides RED being my favorite color, that all who was close to me knew well, ... WORDS REALLY HIT!

Lady In Red
By Chris De Burgh

I've never seen you looking so lovely as you did tonight, I've never seen you shine so bright, ...

Its where I want to be,
But I hardly know this beauty by my side,

ILL NEVER FORGET THE WAY YOU LOOK TONIGHT.

The lady in red,

I love you

As told to me by my husband, Tommy.

January 19, 1987

I t was raining when we were ready to leave Philadelphia. Tommy and Janice, my sister, both asked why we would drive and not take the train. My father and I said that it would be easier and we started for New York. We were going to see my brother in his first Off-Broadway play. The ride was slow and steady. As we approached North New Jersey on the turnpike, the rain began to turn to snow. Traffic slowed somewhat and the snow worsened. Our car slid on the ice. My father put his foot on the brake as we were entering the toll booth . . . as a matter of fact, it was the same toll booth you see on the "Soprano's." As the side of our car was facing traffic, I was knocked unconscious by a commercial van. Everyone except Tommy, was injured. I was hurt more seriously than the others

This was so frightening for everyone in the car. I was out of consciousness, so I did not know what was going on. My father hit his side and fractured his ribs; he was in a lot of pain and was moaning. My sister, Janice, hit her head on the front seat. She was sitting next to me in the back seat and was bleeding. Bianca, my friend was sitting next to Janice. Her body hit the side of the car and she was hurt all over; she was really frightened and was crying. Janice noticed that I was passed out, my head back, leaning on the seat, and making strange noises. She said it sounded like loud snoring. Janice started crying and hugged me and said, "Carol, Carol—sister, my sister."

At that point, my father noticed and turned around and started screaming, "my daughter, my daughter." Then he just cried. Tommy was like an angel; he said to my father, "Rudy, stop, she's going to be alright." Tommy jumped out of the car onto the turnpike and started waving down cars to stop, hoping someone would have a phone. The cars were sliding all over; two almost hit him, but he didn't care. He wanted help for me and finally after about twenty minutes, he found someone with a phone. It was half an hour or so before the ambulance came.

When it finally arrived, it took everyone except Tommy and me to the Elizabeth New Jersey Hospital. I needed to wait for a trauma ambulance because they didn't know what was wrong with me. After waiting approximately 1 hour, the trauma ambulance finally arrived. Because of all the ice, snow, and traffic, it was really hard for them to get me out of the car. They couldn't get the door open. That was the side that was hit. So they had to pry it open and break the glass. They had to take me out straight, which is hard when someone is unconscious. They don't know if your back or neck is broken, so they have to be <u>very careful.</u> As we were traveling to the hospital, my poor husband had to sit in the front seat of the ambulance and watch them work on me. At one point, he saw one of the men shake his head as he was working on me. Tommy tried to get through the gate that separated us. He was like a <u>maniac.</u> The driver tried to calm him down, but it was hard. They had to pull over on the highway and calm Tommy down. Saying to him, "we have to get her to the hospital, she is **NOT DEAD!**

Finally, arriving at the hospital, poor Tommy was waiting alone to find out what was wrong with me. Everyone else was taken to a hospital in Elizabeth, N.J.; they did not need a trauma hospital, thank God. He finally decided to call cousins Michael and Dan, since they were waiting for us to arrive in New York for the play.

He told Michael there had been an accident and after Michael urged him to tell him what was really wrong. Tommy finally said, "Carol is bad, Michael."

Michael said that he and Dan would be right there. Tommy said, "No, wait; you don't have to." Michael just hung up and he and Dan arrived at Newark Hospital within the hour. I was glad to hear that, so Tommy didn't have to be alone. After checking me for over 3 hours, the doctor finally came out and said there was no brain damage, no external bleeding, no damage to the spine. Michael cried. But after some time, they found out that I had suffered a closed-head injury, which, in effect, was a blow to my brain when the impact drove my brain into my skull. I had also suffered a fractured collar bone and fractured pelvis. After a few hours in the emergency trauma unit, the doctors were able to tell my husband that my condition was stable. But there was no way of knowing the outcome until I regained consciousness. I was taken to the hospital's surgical intensive care unit and laid there, comatose for the next **TEN DAYS.** The doctors were **NOT** very optimistic about my recovery. My family began to gather. Tommy and Michael began to sit vigil at my bedside. During this time, my Aunt Ida, a very close aunt of mine, who lived in El Paso, Texas tried to contact me to see how the play went. After three days went by, she thought it was strange that I didn't return her calls since she did leave messages. She called my mother and asked her where I was. My mother could not answer her then. My aunt asked if everything was alright; she had to ask her twice before my mother told her. She was shaken when she heard what had happened, so, she tried to get a flight right away, but could not for a week because of the snow in Newark and New York.

After ten long days, I began to show signs of awakening, doctors began to discuss possibilities of cognitive deficiencies and physical disabilities. They knew I would probably have difficulty walking, talking and eating.

As the days passed, I eventually came in and out of consciousness. The only form of communication I was able to give was at times opening of my eyes or squeezing someone's hand. My family knew I wasn't brain dead but they had no idea just how seriously my brain had been damaged. Tommy and Michael asked if I was going to be okay but the doctors had no answers to give. They just didn't know . . .

Tommy continued to explain to me the long and tedious hospital stay that stretched out over the next twenty days in Newark. I was shocked and found it all very hard to believe. The relief of knowing the answers to the confusing questions I had was satisfying, yet frightening. Intently, I listened to him tell me that I had been in a coma. This actually made me feel better, because I was now sitting up and talking to him. Then Tommy brought to light the details of a time in my life that would change me forever. Not only a change from the injuries I sustained, but also a change in the way I view humanity; I was able to observe those people who were helping to rehabilitate me and others around me.

Prior to the accident, I had an intense interest in health and natural healing. Good diet, exercise and natural supplements had been a way of life for me for almost eight years. Being hospitalized presented me a unique opportunity to make a first-hand observation of the medical approach to healing seriously ill people, of which I was one. The accident and its outcome are the catalyst for writing this story. My real reason for writing it is best said in a quote from Mario Vassi, a great uncle to my husband, **"WHEN ONE HAS LEARNED TO OVERCOME UNPLEASANTNESS IN THE COURSE OF HIS LIFE, THE SHARING OF THE KNOWLEDGE HE HAS GAINED MAY BECOME A SOURCE OF HELP TO OTHERS."**

After many long days of drifting in and out of a coma, I began to stay awake longer, but other complications set in. I was moved to a neurological intensive care unit for even closer monitoring. At this point, some swelling of my brain was showing up on the brain scan. I also developed a severe case of pneumonia. This was the most intense part of my hospital stay. With the pneumonia, came daily suction treatments to clear my lungs. At least three times a day, I had to endure a tube inserted through my nose and down into my lungs.

The doctors had decided to prescribe a ventilator and a drug to reduce the brain swelling. The purpose of the ventilator (a tube put down my throat through my nose) was to increase the amount of oxygen to my brain. I would begin to be awake on a regular basis now and found my situation to be extremely uncomfortable. Tommy explained that it was necessary to take a check out of my blood gases about three times a day, and to do this, a small incision was made at my wrist and then they had to pump the blood out; this, I hear, was excruciating. Along with this, I was constantly being stuck with intravenous needles and other assorted tubes. I managed to keep a pretty good disposition throughout all this discomfort, and I was still getting a huge amount of support from my family. According to my husband, the nursing staff had taken a special interest in me. Their care was constant, twenty-four hours a day; especially, the nurse, Peter, who would always talk to me and brush my hair.

After many days of this grueling routine, the ventilator tube was finally removed and I was able to communicate with my family and people in the hospital. In the beginning, I spoke very little and mostly what I said was incoherent, not easily understood by everyone. It was around this time that my cousin Michael, my husband and my Aunt Ida were starting to take notice of what I would talk about. It's funny how things happen; she decided to move to Philadelphia after all of this. She lives one block from me now. My family noticed when I would wake up from my coma, I spoke of conversations with deceased family members and would ask questions about them. At this point

I lost a considerable amount of weight and everyone was concerned with trying to get me to eat. I couldn't eat and when I could, it was very little. When the pneumonia finally cleared, and the swelling subsided, the doctors began to talk about sending me to a rehabilitation hospital closer to home. An attempt to make arrangements for this move was made by the hospital staff, but the idea was rejected by the hospital in Philadelphia.

I was moved, instead, from the intensive care unit to a private room with a twenty-four hour day nurse. As I became clearer and more awake, I began to notice more pain, especially where I had broken my collar bone. They had this contraption that was put on my shoulders and down my back; it was very heavy so I couldn't move. My family said I kept trying to get it off of me; it was obviously very uncomfortable. The discomfort from lying in bed for so long had heightened and it became harder to lie still. Some attempts were made at the most basic physical therapy, but I grew extremely uncooperative. I continued this pattern of being in and out of awareness. The doctors tried again to have me moved. This time the plan was accepted and plans were made for moving me.

Tommy explains to me that we took a long and uncomfortable ambulance ride to Magee Rehabilitation Hospital in Philadelphia. This is where I first started to realize I was injured. As for the time beginning with the accident to the move to Philadelphia, I have no recollection except for what I have been told. Michael told me how difficult it was for him when I left Newark Hospital; he had been with me the whole month every single day. So when they put me in the ambulance, he just stood there watching me and he said I waved and said, "I love you Michael, thanks." He cried. This was a TRAUMATIC experience for my cousin. He needed to scream at times or cry. So to make it more bearable for himself, he wrote what he was doing and how he felt about the experience almost every day, which helped him cope with what was happening, a little easier. I would like to share this with you. After I was home about a month, Michael asked me if I would like to read what he wrote about my stay in the hospital. I told him I wasn't ready. It frightened me to read about it. But after some time went by, I was curious and ready. So he mailed it all to me. I lay in bed one night and read it all. It took a long time because I was crying the whole time. Not because it frightened or depressed me, but because it was so beautiful reading what Michael wrote. First of all, he writes beautifully. Plus, it was so strange . . . I felt like I knew <u>everything</u> he had experienced. Nobody at this point had told me all the details.

Tommy & I in Virginia Beach 1979

Daughters with Daddy
Janice, Renee and Me

Mommy with Her Children
Renee, Mommy
Janice, Rudy and Me

Michael & I with Dan
Nephew Dante In Front at Aunt Louise's
Easter Sunday 2003 and it was my BIRTHDAY 50 years old

Tommy & I on our Wedding Day (May 17, 1981)

Janice, Dad, Mom, Renee, and Rudy . . . We
lost mom and dad ☹

Tommy's Family
Mom, Dad, Sister Lorraine, Paul, Laina (Lorraine's Child)
"We lost Mom & Dad" ☹

Aunts & Uncles
Uncle Ralph, Mom, Uncle Dante, Aunt Louise, Dad,
Aunt Elaine, Uncle John, Aunt Carol, Uncle Sam, Aunt Toni

We . . . lost Uncle Ralph, Mommy, Uncle Dante, Aunt Louise,
Daddy, Uncle John, Uncle Sam & Aunt Toni . . . . So many ☹

"Cousins"
John, Jan, Rudy, Michele, Gina, Anthony, Bobby,
Karen, Emilio, Fred, Margaret Angela, Frank,
Michael, Me, Tom, Renee, Maureen & Chris

Michele "Catching Bouquet"
Lorraine & Maureen Buckley, who I lost contact years ago ☹
Looking on Roseanne
Bella left, who we lost ☹
Karen & Aunt Carol right

With Aunt Jean
Lauren & Renee

Family dancing at my wedding
Cousin Mark, Janice, Uncle Mike (who we lost),
Uncle Ralph (who we lost)
Bobby's back with Celeste

Dan, Mari, Friend, Michael, Maureen, Warren

Honeymoon
"Acapulco"

Honeymoon
Tom caught me without make up . . .
Couldn't do that today

MICHAEL'S JOURNAL

"Nothing is as it appears to be even
when it is certain." Dr. Joy

1-19-87

T alking with Maureen (Michael's sister) on the phone waiting for your arrival. We got into a deep conversation about life-/ death—feelings about Dad, spirituality, and fear of exploring and entering the spiritual world. Excited to see you, I went out and did a little food shopping. Special treats for you—you and your diet. During my phone conversation with Maureen, another call came through. I was watching the snow fall from my window. It was Tommy; "There's been an accident." I got the number from Tommy; clicked back to Maureen and told her to hold on until I got back to her.

At this moment my connection to Carol was direct. Called Tommy; he was in the emergency ward at Newark University Hospital. I told him I'd be right there—he said wait. I asked and pushed for details. He said, "it's bad, Michael." Dan and I rushed to the train—it felt like minutes from NY to the hospital in Newark. Tom was alone with a bag of all of Carol's possessions. Carol was still in emergency.

My first tears came when the doctor came out and said there seemed to be no brain damage, no internal bleeding and no damage to the spine. All we had was unconscious Carol.

Called Maureen and she relayed it to other family members.

At this moment in time, my focus was on helping Carol to heal.

Finally, they let Tommy and me in to see Carol. Like sleeping beauty—silent—eyes closed—glowing with life energy, yet on a level unfamiliar to us.

> No hand squeezes
> No gestures
> Still . . .

Talking quietly, turned into pleading, begging for Carol to come back. It was a nightmare come true.

Dan was outside in the waiting area acting as a strong support for both Tommy and me.

. . . this night was the beginning of a process that accentuated all of our strengths and fears.

Somehow Carol never seemed that far away to me. I remember seeing my dad in a coma—he was moving to the other side. Carol in a coma—seemed to be fighting for life; even though she was perfectly still, I felt her energy overpowering the entire room.

Carol, you are truly a wonderful person.

Dan left at one point and Tommy and I continued our journey into the night. We made many visits to Carol. In her silent way, she responded:

You radiate warmth
   beauty and
   love.
Your silence hurts Tommy.
Your glow comforts us.

A few hours of sleep in the ugly room.

1-20-87

I have a major mix for "Change in Me." When I arrive home, I cry, I scream, I lie on my bed in awe of the whole situation. Carol, come back—you have to!

I never made it to the studio. Dan went and did our work. My world was consumed with Carol. How could I make myself stronger so that I could help? I needed to be strong in order to give at this level.

Feeling a little afraid to be alone, Warren came over to comfort me. During my sleeping period 1:00 a.m. Tommy called. Carol opened her eyes and made some sounds. It was such great news. I called the studio. A surge of phone calls and absolute electric energy circled the entire universe.

1-21-87

Tom and I get Carol to stay awake for a little while. Now with a respirator and wires all over, Carol says, "I have to go to the bathroom." Before I could recognize her request, Tommy and I guessed everything but . . .

It's like some foreign language using hands. Very similar to sign language. Precise, as in a ballet. Gestures appreciated in a new way from my eyes. Every movement was a miracle.

After our moments with Carol, I left with Dan.

1-22-87

Major snow storm!

Many days in the hospital. My life purpose was to bring Carol back.

I became an integral part of a most miraculous process. An opportunity to feel my spiritual energy take over. Verbal communication was slow—if nothing at all.

Love is the answer.
Love is what I began to feel stronger than ever before.

Carol, you have taught me what the words "unconditional love" mean.

My focus made me stronger. My strength helped Carol to grow.

The tubes seem so uncomfortable.
wires
beepers
tape on your face
your arms.

Oh God, help me stay strong.
- using a suction hose to take out mucus
- holding Carol down while she had her IV put in.

Pneumonia meant more mucus
    more suction.

The more aware Carol became, the happier we were, yet, the more pain Carol felt.

I had to work on balance
    on priorities
    on understanding.

The body—WOW!

1/25-27

Many questions??? From nurses. Not sure of answers.
    Carol—where are you?
    When did you get here?
        Etc.

Carol's response in face
        hands
        shoulders.

M—Carol—do you know who I am?
C—Of course.
M—I thought so, but the nurses just wanted to see.
C—They're full of shit!

Man calling from bed.

Doctor/nurse help me!

C—Call Dr. Columbia.
M—What should I ask him?
C—I need Vitamin C and B.

C—I love you and Dan a lot.
C—How's Warren (a friend)?
M—He's fine; he's in Ohio
C—(Questioning face) Why?
    etc.

C—Mari? (friend)
C—Jeremy? (Mari's son)

Alone with Carol and Aunt Annie (Carol's mother)
Points to herself.
Spells out (LOVE) with index finger
Points to me.

Took toothbrush from nurse and scrubbed mouth totally energized.

C—I've been here before.
M—I bet you have Carol. You know you're psychic.
C—I know.

1/28

(Denise Nanni, Aunt Ida, Dante, Louise)
  - tube out
  - oxygen mask
  - sat up in chair
  - brushed teeth herself
  - ate cup of rice
  - drank cup of water

1/29

  - nurse (Tess)
  - long sleep (9:00 p.m.-2:00 p.m.)
  - sat up in chair

- woke up by the time Tom arrives (4:00 p.m.)
- smiles
- laughs about obnoxious man in next bed.

And where are you now, Carol?
You know who we are.
You know what you need.
You know how you feel.
And where are you now, Carol?
I stand here talking with you.
I love seeing you.
You hold me tight/close.
Kiss my forehead.
I am with you
and where are we?
All questions answered
except where are we?
Such inspiration.
I see you as always.
Your expression so natural
        so Carol.
I begin to look at you in your world.
I want you to tell me about it.
I know you are traveling.
I know you are gaining new information.
You do not seem afraid.
You are stronger by the moment.
You will not lose.
You can only gain—strength
                    insight
                    power.
You have gone so deep inside yourself.
And I can never doubt you are learning more out of life.
You are normal to me.

You just need at some point to come to our plane so that we may continue to understand your energy.

You are truly a wonderful person

1/30/87—Friday

- – a lot of sleep
- Aunt Ida with Carol (evening)
- – 2 glasses of water
- – feeling no pain

C— I feel sentimental. Asks about family. Who cheated who; beginning with Uncle Mike. Asks for grandmom.
I—what happens in January?
C—your birthday, January 15th!
Great work, Carol!

M—Carol, why are you sleeping so much? You're so tired.
C—I'm high.
M—From what?
C—All the drugs they're giving me.

1/31/87

(On train to Newark)
I spent one whole day and night away—not physically seeing you. I think of you, your progress, your healing process. Moment by moment you live inside yourself surfacing from time to time to time . . .

You are a healer.
You are a strong person.
You believe in unconditional love.
You give
And you will continue to receive in abundance!
love
health
success and
<u>happiness</u>

1/31/87

See tubes out.
Carol pulls my face to hers.
Holds me/my forehead, touching her warm cheek and says . . .
    "I felt love."

My response was . . .
    "I know."

And we stayed in this position for a bit—white light energy glowed inside and out.

Carol is healing. Renee (Carol's sister) stood beside the bed. It was a special moment for me. Another one in this life!

When I saw Carol today, she looked so delicate like a hand-carved marionette. Her face was free of tubes and tape. She was fed cereal/yogurt/peas (which I helped eat), etc. She looked so peaceful yet so unsure of her situation. She is getting stronger moment by moment. She is healing.

2/1/87

AN INTENSIVE DAY 11:00 a.m.-8:00 p.m. FOREVER

We shopped for Carol at the health food store on Prince Street.

When we arrived, Tommy and I found her sitting (slouched) in a chair, eyes wide open, checking out her situation. She was full of questions, requesting honest, straight-forward answers. She mainly focused on relationships, marriage, sexuality. She seems to have visited with a lot of people. Aunt Agusta, Grandmom, her mom, dad, aunts, uncle, friends. She singled out people; couples and felt close, yet distant.

C—"Many people have a lot to get together."

Through this day, she built a trust in Tommy and me. Talking about so many personal things. She sang some songs along with the radio. She laughed and had us laughing.

There were moments when Carol would close off. Dazed in space or close her eyes. Just shut off. She said it was fear. She was afraid to be happy because it meant sadness was close. She recalled her childhood . . . "whenever my father was home and happy, I knew there was going to be sadness because he would always leave us. One time I was in the car with Aunt Louise and my mom. Aunt Louise was laughing and the next minute, she was crying from something my mother had said.

Carol kept giving examples of why she was afraid of happiness/of life/of facing herself. Some were real stories, some perhaps dreams.

Carol was intensely searching for truth! "I need to know myself before I can know anyone else. I need to love myself . . ."

Carol has been away in a sleep for fourteen days—carol has been inside herself!

Heal yourself, sweet cousin, and acknowledge your power and beauty.

I feel like I've been tripping for days (gestures hands to head) like who . . . who . . . who . . . ?

I feel like everyone just thinks I'm strange.

Have you two ever slept together?

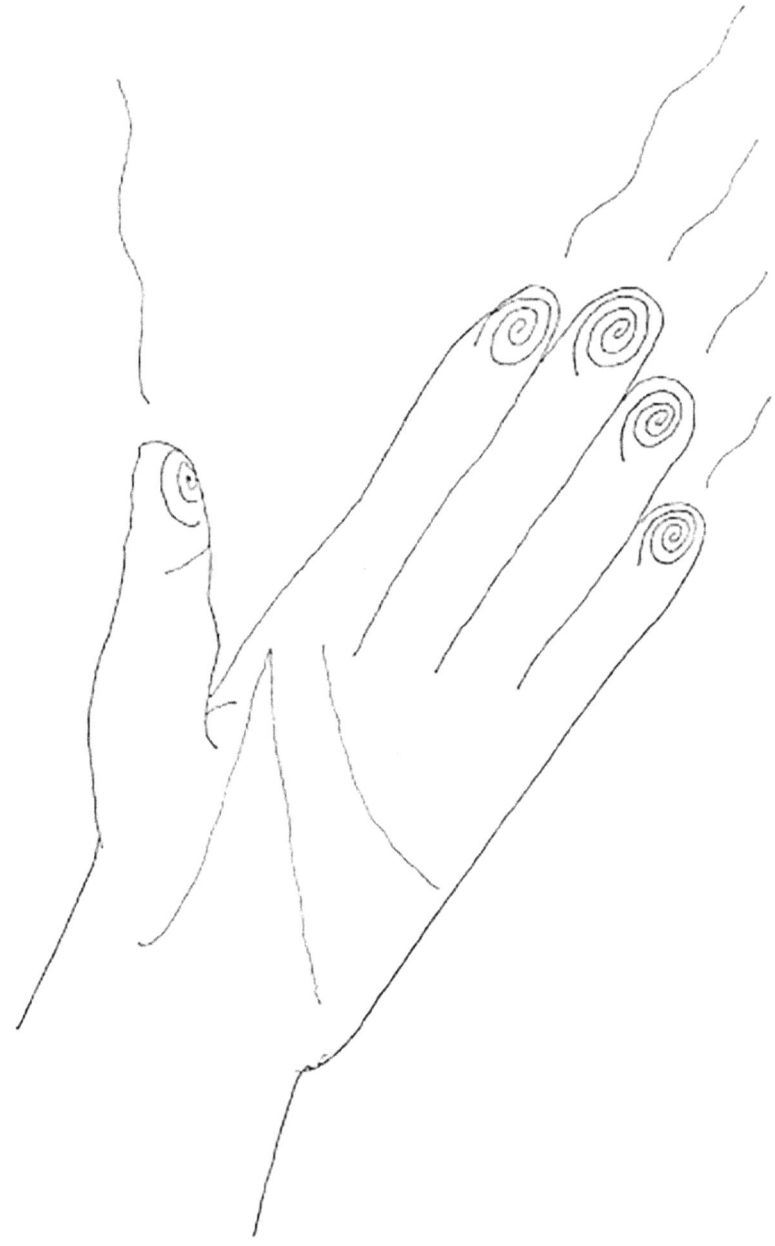

. . . drawing done by Michael as he was
sitting and looking at Carolann

. . . drawing done by Michael as he was
sitting and looking at Carolann

. . . drawing done by Michael as he was
sitting and looking at Carolann

LEFT HAND HEALING

. . . drawing done by Michael as he was
sitting and looking at Carolann

Why can't I remember?

I know I've been here before.

I'm from a black family.

I want twins, 1 boy/1 girl.

Why do we have to be "married"? Why can't we just love each other and be friends?

"Marriage" (gestures quotation marks) has too much emphasis in peoples' lives.
- Related a lot of her sadness to her parents
- Her parents had a sad marriage

Carol, don't be afraid of your power and beauty!

2/6/87

Today we moved to room 222, G Blue, 3:00 p.m.

The move seemed about 3 days overdue, but in the hospital patience is a virtue one learns.

At times it feels like one could fight with the doctors and nurses, but that wouldn't be fair to Carol. The more we care and communicate, the more we get back. One thing is they saw our concern and constant eye so they too pushed for the positive direction.

Carol seems very anxious at times. (Who wouldn't?).

"My body aches."

"My hinee hurts."

"Everyone is forcing me to do things."

"They're killing people in here." (Man across from her bed; his family stands around with rubber gloves on.)

"Patient (Robert) yelling, "reefer."

Carol wants out. (Who wouldn't?)

. . . and here we sit. Aunt Ida, Nurse Barbara, me and Carol (sleeping) in Room 222, G Blue.

"I want to move to New York."

"I need a change."

"I want to make cookies," "Carol's cookies (i.e. Barbara's brownies)."

"I want babies."

Everything Carol wanted, she still wants now more than ever. Carol go get it All!

2/7/87

Evening (night-time)

Tommy and I had a talk about Carol.

T—Do you think Carol will ever be the same?

M—No.

This doesn't disappoint me. I feel this is Carol's reality and she is going through major changes in her lifetime. (The best is yet to come.)

People say: "Will Carol be normal again?/that's not like Carol!:/That's not Carol in the bed." Of course that's Carol. Look at her. That is Carol and Carol will continue to heal and grow better than ever before. Not as my cousin but as a friend, partner, and twin soul from many lifetimes ago. Carol is a spiritual being.

Don't be afraid, Carol (as I tell myself the same thing). We ended our conversation with good feelings and worked on a plan of action for Tommy's peace of mind. Tomorrow we go in with good positive energy, unconditional love, and healing powers.

2/8/87

A great day. Going through any and every emotion. Carol is surrounded by Aunt Ida, Tommy, Dan, Gwyendeline (nurse), Michael. We made major strides. Carol made major strides. She reached a moment of relaxation, peaceful radiant love surrounds the bed. As Carol slowly sipped her soup through a flexible straw. Each sip was such a delight to all of us.

Patience
Love
Understanding
Unconditional love.

She fought.
I focused.
She fought.
We focused.

Together we put nourishment into her body.
Our goal at this moment is to give nourishment to a healing body.

A few specific moments.
Gwen said even if it takes her eight hours to drink a protein drink, that would be fine. A sip all through the day and she'll finish it. No need to force it.
I followed her advice and was quite pleased with the process.

Massage me . . .
My hands
My feet
My back
My shoulders
My belly, etc.

We had our hands all over Carol. Love is the answer.

Michael: Carol, why can't you eat?
Carol: Please don't force me.
Michael: I won't force you. Just can you tell me why?
Carol: My stomach hurts.
I need a massage.
I'll eat in five minutes. Please don't force me.
Michael: Carol, do you know why your stomach hurts?
You are taking a lot of medication and
your stomach is upset and food may help.
Carol: No, don't force me.
Michael: You know you need nourishment. You tell me that all
the time.

Carol: Massage me.
Michael: Carol, what would you like? You need to eat!
Carol: Soup.

(A word from heaven) and on the tray there was soup.

I added the mashed potatoes and squash (puree) to the soup and,
slowly in Carol's timing, helped her focus and finish her soup.

What a major achievement.

When she finished, Tommy came back into room and was so pleased
and proud. He embraced her, resting his head silently against hers.

Aunt Ida left the room to call Aunt Louise and Dan and I left. I looked at the lovers and saw something so tender and beautiful. The moment was precious. Treasure it and go on. There's so much to life. A lot more to learn and live.

Carol is healing.
I can feel it.
I am healing.

Aunt Ida and Tommy arrived home a few hours later. Of course the imagined gridlock was at the end of the Holland Tunnel. And it snowed and I delivered Aunt Ida to the Path at 8:30 a.m. (NYC rush hour).

All in all, it was a magnificent time/every moment of the way.

2/9/87

I am thinking of you today, Carol. I'm presently in Gary's studio dubbing tapes (40) for our new project. I want to take all that you are teaching me and celebrate life. I am very quiet today. I feel so fulfilled. Lauren and Warren called and talked a lot. I felt silent watching the snow outside. It all makes sense to me. I love you.

2/10/87

Carol, today you had no IV, no tubes, no prods or pointers. You pulled it out during the night. We can keep it out if you eat. All we have to do is eat. Also today will be your first day in therapy on the "TILT TABLE."

Then an X-ray for your back. Time to put the IV back but Tommy spoke with the Doctor and if you eat, we can keep it out.

My goal for the moment is to make sure you eat dinner.
We did it!
Moment by moment.

2/11/87

"Do my other body"

- "I have jet lag."
- "I have car lag."

Are you and Tommy dancing?
rub my toes
massage my feet

What an active day, Carol. Tommy and I arrived quite wiped out. Feeling physically sick ourselves. Through the day, each of your achievements helped us regain strength. Belief in myself helped me believe in your recovery.

New goal was to get you out of Newark!

We did it, Carol—tomorrow at 10:30.

You were so much fun today. A lot of strain on the back, but a lot of love and fulfillment of my spirit. Every move painful or not touched my deepest feelings with love. Tommy and I took a lunch break in Manhattan "Life Café." On the way back, we were sick and tired of Newark and the ugly ride to the hospital. We laughed like crazy people. Totally clear about our direction in life . . . your recovery! When we arrived, I pulled in a giant breath.

In therapy today, they had you sit on a mat on the floor in front of a mirror and look at yourself. It was very difficult for you to do. You squirmed and complained and slid around. Tommy left and I sat behind the curtain as not to distract you. You scream, "Tommy, Michael, help me," several times. We were helping you because after your workout of rolling and rolling, your perception changed. It was difficult and you did it. You're great, Carol.

And the whole day progressed from that; moment by moment we reached our new goals for this specific day.

2/12/87

Arrive at the Hospital early with Dan and Tommy.

Carol is awake. More aware than ever.

Says that she kept the nurses moving all night. "It's a wonder they don't throw me out of here."

Asks if the accident she was in was bad? "Yes."

(Asks question during a TV show where Chita Rivera was talking about her recovery from a car accident.)

Note of Feb. 11th

Dan arrives home from Philly saddened a bit by Pileggi's (where I worked) and family.

DAN,
You are a special person and I love you.

Carol's spirits stay high. She talks for the first time on the phone to Aunt Toni and Aunt Ida.

Says to Dan, "I'll have to learn to make small talk again."

Carol, you seem today to accept your situation.

Acceptance is a great thing to help you get stronger. Barbara stops in to say good-bye. Dr. Lax stops in to look. Serious, gives his interpretation of the new brain scans. He doesn't even acknowledge Carol's leaving: at least to say good-bye and wish her well (sleeping or not).

Carol is aware of energy. Lax calls Tommy out and he comes into the room serious. I only have what I have and know what I see and regardless of brain scans, Carol Ann needs positive energy, not heavy-handed, heavy-headed, serious (maximum damage) energy.

She sleeps through our discussing the scans and awakes all disoriented. It seems to be a pattern that slowly gets shorter and shorter. Finally when she fights to keep awake, she is aware once again of life and time.

She is preparing for a journey to Philadelphia. Fresh air from hospital door to ambulance door for the first time in over three weeks. I tell her to breathe it in when she hits the air. Before they put her on the stretcher, I ask her for a hug. I lie in her arms; she hugs me and thanks me for the help and tells me she loves me. WOW!

Onto the stretcher, down the hall with two men in blue, Tommy, Dan and I. As we wait for the elevator, she says she feels like she's in a TV movie. Down to the desk to check her out of the hospital. She thanks me for my red sweats. "I love you, Carol."

It's difficult for me to detach myself, but I know the time is near. I go out to the ambulance and she looks at me as they put her inside all strapped up with blankets. I wave and my eyes fill with tears.

Bye, Carol Ann—

God keep you strong on your new phase to recovery. Keep strong and work until you yourself are satisfied with your accomplishments.

Be everything you want to be—you have another chance at life. Go for it!

I hear from Tommy that the ride was rough. Mari meets you at Magee. They immediately give you a little test. With a paper and pen, you write. No one can understand, so you tell them:

"When you love somebody, it's the best."

VIT B

Complex

B + B

. . . Michael handed me a paper and pen after
I was in Magee Rehab and I wrote this

. . . then a doctor, I think Larry Norn, asked me as soon as
I arrived at Magee to write whatever I felt and I wrote . . .

"WHEN YOU LOVE SOMEONE, IT'S THE BEST ☺"

It was really hard for them to understand, but they got it.

. . . Suppose to read "Vit. B Complex" B12 looks like BoB

They say I was making a "V" with my fingers pointing at Tom. Making sure he was taking his vitamins. Tom said he looked pretty ragged. Didn't sleep good for 7 days . . . Wouldn't leave my side.

There is love all around you, now take it in and love yourself so that you can truly heal and live a new, powerful existence.

In Philly, you will have to once again adjust to a new space and to new faces. In a few days, you'll orient yourself, focus on healing and get well.

You have certainly inspired my life. I miss you. You are on my mind when I wake in the morning, when I rest in the night, all through the day and even in my dreams. You have become more precious to me than ever imagined. This time in our lifetime is very valuable. It is something that we had to go through to go onto the next phase in life. You helped me overcome many fears. You helped me see what it is to focus and succeed (even in the simplest of ways). You taught me to love unconditionally and you helped me believe and love myself. Thanks, Carol!

2/17/87

Carol, I spoke with you today on the phone. You sound so clear.

2/18/87 (Wed.)

It's six days now that Carol was transferred to Magee. I'll be in Philly today for three special occasions: 1) to see Carol; 2) to drop off Masters and Remick; 3) to see my family (whom I haven't seen since the accident and before).

Carol, when I walked into your room you were asleep. I am with Maureen and Dan. I look at you, unsure it is you. Covered so gently with a beautiful comforter (I guess it's from home). You look a bit thinner and still radiant! Magee is so full of working-healing (on this plane) energy. I walk towards you and wake you. You are happy to see us and begin telling stories of your time at Magee, about your therapy work. How they pinch you with pins and how they have you move your fingers. It all seems so simple to you and watching you in your new environment, I realize it is helping you tremendously. We all talked for at least one hour. Then change space with Gilda, Julie and Sharon. The three of us visit the cafeteria for tea. It is packed with wheelchairs, beds with rollers, and is completely organized. Everyone is rehabilitating themselves. It is full of love and life and hope. Janice comes down in about one hour and we all come back to your room.

It's time to eat. First, the toilet—Dan and I walk you over, step by step. For the first time, I feel you help with your own weight. Janice and I put you on the potty. This is a first for me. I guess it helped you today because you walked slowly up and back on the parallel bars. I am so satisfied with your recovery. We then sit in the TV room for dinner. (Dan made you chicken soup). And there you are surrounded by me, Maureen, Dan, Hon, Janice, Sharon, Aunt Gilda, Julie, and then enters cousin John. You say: "it's like a cousins' party." It is, and it was so much fun. Incredible loving energy once again fills the entire room. Oh Carol, you teach us to love. After dinner (I hid a few zucchini under the turkey slices), you go for a short wheelchair walk with Maureen and Tommy. Your dad comes in and we visit a bit. When I come back to your room, you are asleep with Mo and Rudy sitting by your bed. So peaceful. It's almost time to leave and you awake with anxiety. So, Tommy and Janice begin the "get Carol comfortable" routine. We all go in peace. God bless you, Carol!

Off to Bittern Place to see everyone.

My thoughts of you are powerful. People seem impatient with your progress. Your anxiety is holding your healing process back at least one month. "how about anti-depressants?" you and Tommy and Doc have a discussion in the morning. You decided to go with drugs. They will help you focus. I feel if you've come this far, you can take the time you need to complete the healing, but life-pressure calls. So I feel if you cleansed your body once, you can do it again. Use the drug and please Carol, clean it out as soon as possible. Your inner functions are so pure. Now your spiritual powers are more vivid. I hope I can help you join the two forces together so that you realize what a powerful person you really are. Beyond what anyone and everyone thinks of Cousin Carol. You're the strongest, I have ever seen!

2/19/87

Back in New York city (spoke with Tom this morning from my mom's). He told me about the anti-depressant. He sounds much happier than yesterday. To him, this is moving forward. I respect his decision. I will support and help you get that poison out of your body as soon as they allow us to do it . . . ! I have learned many things from you; "patience" is one of them. Thanks!

I saw my healer today. He arrived in NYC on Monday for a few weeks.

(Healer): you are so bright. He closes his eyes and feels my energy. He opens his eyes. "there is someone close to you who is ill. Someone very close, a soul-mate. How are they now?" I tell him a bit about who you are. "Carol has chosen to stay on. It's as if at one point, she could die or live on. She chose to live and you were there to see it. She is a giver. She doesn't really take time to receive. She is too busy organizing things to please other people. This situation is created by Carol to draw full energy to herself so she can experience people giving totally! Only in this situation will she fully experience the abundance of love around her. Her right side seems weaker, more painful. This is her "mother" side. She has needed and desired the love of her mother for a long time in her life. Her anxiety is her nervous system's (a neurological) reaction to her brain trauma. Slowly it dissipates.

He acknowledged me for being part of the healing process. Carol chose the whole situation. You were able to give her love unconditionally. She needed that to feel stronger. He really helped me appreciated and acknowledge your recovery. He tells me to give you orange. ORANGE! ORANGE! Energy to root your feet to the earth in your powerful way. Enjoy life, Carol!

5·2·81 *drawn on my way to see Carol.*

... drawing done by Michael as he was
sitting and looking at Carolann

. . . drawing done by Michael as he was
sitting and looking at Carolann

CAROLANN PUT ON SOME MAKE UP TODAY.

. . . drawing done by Michael as he was
sitting and looking at Carolann

3/2/87

On the Amtrak,
on my way to see you,
some thoughts go through my mind. I see you changing, entering into that world (this world) that everyone questioned whether or not you'd be part of again?
Carol all I pray for now is that you do enter in a new light. Life is new for you. Live it in the way you need to feel fulfilled. No need to pretend. Life has offered you to live again.

Everyone has been given time to feel their weaknesses and strengths without you to build the belief in themselves—the beliefs you worked so hard to introduce to them. Your presence was respected while you were away. Your energy alive. Your words had stronger meaning to all who know you. I realized how deeply you touched the lives you walked through. Everyone wanted Carol back to normal, including me. Except, I wanted you back, not like before, but in fact stronger than before, with more focus on yourself, your inner beauty,
your spiritual energy,
your bright, positive light
which shines from your body even as you lay unconscious.
You are back, Carol.
Trust that you made a decision to continue on life's path.
Enjoy yourself.
Enjoy your own self.
And from this will be an abundance of unconditional love for all who want it.
You are truly wonderful!

3/2/87 (train on my way back to NYC)

Saw Aunt Ida, Maureen, Michael-Ann, Aunt Ann, Tommy; later,
Janice, Uncle Rudy and Renee.
Carol was very chatty today.
Making lots of sense.
Looking well.
I kind of ignored everyone because I am in awe of the situation.

When she goes to eat in the TV room, Tommy talks with the Doctor.
He comes back in the room a bit concerned and depressed. Doc
says Carol may find it hard to organize; she may ramble on and not
remember. She may never be the same; she may get very angry in the
middle of a department store, etc. PLEASE . . .

I defensively stood up for Carol's rights as a human being. As a
"normal" human being. She is a new person; she will learn to relax, to
slow down and to come into her heart space if she needs to; meditation,
yoga, music, and many other forms of focus that maybe the doctor
overlooks. If Carol does, in fact, have these "disabilities," we "normal"
people think she has, then we will learn to live with them. And more
important than that is that Carol learns and understands to accept
who she is and live it to her absolute fullest!

It's not fair to treat a disability as if it were a sorrowful situation or
as if it puts us in a martyred position. We as all human beings have
the freedom to choose our own destiny, and if life is becoming one
big sacrifice then you are not helping the person you feel concerned
about.

Carol, I support you in your healing process.
I support you in your new time of life.
I support your new ways and the only time I personally will interfere
is if I feel you would do yourself or someone else physical harm.

I cannot imagine such a thing would ever happen because of everyone, I know your respect and love for the body and its functions is 100% sincere.

You are truly fabulous and I love you. Amen! Go for it!

You mentioned writing a book today:
　　ways to help in therapy
　　massage
　　food
　　physical contact
　　to relax
　　have children around your pets
　　positive energy

Tommy said tonight after Aunt Ida, Maureen and I all disagreed with the Doctor's visit. "I jut block you all out; I know how I feel." For this, my inner response is "so do we all." For each person, it is a personal experience. None greater than the next and each one of us has a belief system and a heart that feels and I respect each one's connection to Carol. For Tommy, it seems endless; your husband, lover, and friend. And to me, as I take distance form you, I see your development and feel your healing process in a wider scale, in a wider range—outside the perimeters of your room at Magee, outside the perimeters of your space and life in Philadelphia. But instead, your beaming energy as it helps the universe to appreciated the powerful gifts you have and give to others.

Cousin Michelle feels we have a bond from many roots ago. Carol, Michael, and Michelle, I can't wait for the three of us to be united and expand our knowledge and love.

3/3/87 (thoughts after our visit yesterday)

M—Three things you miss the most being in the hospital for 43 days.

C— 1. Tommy
    2. my house
    3. work

M—Pileggi's

C—not necessarily. I just miss being busy. I don't like just being here in bed. I want to be busy, to work everyday.

You talked about writing a book
-   find a ghost writer
-   begin to gather thoughts and notes
-   begin to discipline yourself in your own creative personal line of work/teach and write
-   share your experience and wisdom with people

you have touched many hearts in your circle of family and friends.

Widen the circle; extend it to the universe because you truly have the potential to reach millions of people who need people like you?

After our visit last night, I went to have some dinner with Maureen, Emilio, and Michael-Ann. I got a bottle of apple juice; in the cap it read:
    "Tears are summer showers to the soul."

You told me you cried a lot. I said crying is good. A good, healthy emotional release. This message in the cap says it all.

3/8/87

(Afternoon on 8th Street; walk to Washington Square)

"Amtrak Blues," a song sung by Alberta Hunter

I'm on Amtrak, but I ain't blue.
I'm on my way to see you.
Home today on 8th Street. Haven't seen you there since Cousin Fred (after birthday party, left Spring St. at 11:07, ran to buy a tofu pie, hopped a cab, got the 11:30 Amtrak, and here I sit on my way to see you as planned).
Many spirit guides lead me as I go. Schedule timing!

Newark stop . . .
. . and onward.
"Change In Me" is on my headset.

Dan and I talked about "Doctors."

May '87

They don't involve you enough in your own recovery. They know people are afraid of CHANGE so they give them prescriptions to help solve their problems. This doesn't give the patient the freedom to change according to the natural flow of what they're really confronted with.

- All based on fear of change.

Sat., July 25, 1987

There is so much more . . . I look over what I have written and I begin to remember other images and stories . . . things outside of myself . . . concerns for the family, friends, phones, etc. for whatever reasons, these pages are what my heart and mind chose to write. I could expand on a lot of the ideas, but as I read I feel the true meaning shines through—YOU.

All the other stuff; anger with Rudy or my family or Tommy's family, etc. did not take the start role. You were the star and I wanted to help you continue to shine. I saw during that time how much you meant to people (both family and friends). I saw how much your "light helped in guiding others to see." People missed you so . . . and what I see is that you were still giving . . . in a new way. I was given so many simple messages, which made me see your personal power even more than before. That big question . . . everyone's concern . . . Will Carol ever be the same? Every time we go through anything, we "change" if we let ourselves. I still believe that "the same" is the past. Of course your essence is the same, but you are a better, stronger, and wiser person. Each time we go inside ourselves, we come out with new information. Our person grows and changes, and hopefully accepts who they really are. You were a spirit guide for many, and through your experience you can and did take us all further into a new realization about life. It's obvious; look at Ann (Carolann's mother) and Jean (Michael's mom) and Hon (Carol called Tommy "Hon," so did many others, it rubbed off ☺), and Renee (Carolann's sister), etc. some people let you in . . . and they are blessed for that because even in your coma state—you were GIVING!

Keep building your NEW SELF. The Carol we all know and love is still here—her energy and light is here forever!

M

Michael & I as Children, 3-4 yrs old

Me & Michael, After
Injury 1988 or 1989

Tommy & I fooling around . . . Cousin Michael did for
us . . . such an ARTIST HE IS ☺

. . . Michael asked me before I read his journal . . . "Do you remember anything when you were in your coma?"

. . . the only thing I remember was Tommy's face very, very close to mine, just staring at me. When Tommy wasn't there, Michael was standing about six inches away from me. Holding my hand and constantly speaking to me. I also heard my sister Renee's voice a lot but never saw her.

When I told Michael this, he couldn't believe it. He was constantly speaking to me—Tommy was constantly staring at me—Renee couldn't come close—she just would talk to Michael form the door.

Then I mentioned to Michael and Renee . . . I didn't know why I felt this but I was going to write a book. I never thought of ever writing a book in my life. So feeling this was strange to me. When I told them, Renee screamed then started to cry. "Why are you crying," I said. "Michael told me when you were in a coma, don't worry, Renee, Carolann's going to be alright. She's going to write a book and teach us." One thing I definitely believe is when someone is in a coma— they can hear. So if you tell them positive things, it will help them and stay with them.

My cousin Michael helped me <u>so, so</u> much. He constantly told me good positive things to make me stronger . . . Thank you, Michael, I love you so much!

. . . what happened to me is known as TRAUMA in the medical profession. Long before there were trauma centers to treat people who suffered injuries like these, there was not much hope that they would live, let alone return to normal life.

Now medical science has found a way to facilitate an almost complete recovery. What they have not been able to follow through with is a way to treat these people with a degree of respect as human beings. This is TRAUMATIC for the patient. To say how the doctors and nurses treat the patients . . . **PHYSICALLY,** they do great things. I went from lying in bed—wheeling myself in a wheelchair—walking between two bars on both sides—then a walker—just walking normally . . . being just a little off-balance. Falling at times, so I had to walk slow and not when I was tired. It took me a few years to get it right. Till today, if I'm tired "balance is off" ☹

MENTALLY, they treat you like you're really stupid and if the patient had no confidence about themselves prior to the accident, they'd really be in trouble.

They shouldn't ask such dumb questions. They should just talk to the patients like they're normal and have normal conversations with them . . . like for instance, "what's your name?" "what's your mother's name?" "what year is it?" etc. they should say "these questions may sound stupid to you, but you had a brain injury and I need to see how your brain is working." Instead, I had no idea why they were asking me, and I felt really stupid like I was retarded and I just wanted to go home.

Another thing they did was walk in and say "eat this or take this pill." Bedside manner is very, very important. I was having stomach pain and nausea for about two weeks. I couldn't eat anything for all that time. I lost thirty pounds. I cannot afford to lose <u>any weight</u>. I'm normally a very thin person . . . at 110 lbs. I knew then that taking all those pills every was making me sick. They handed me twelve pills a day <u>ALL AT ONCE</u>.

And they would say, "you have to take these!" I would ask what they were for, but they would just roll their eyes and walk out of the room!

At first, I would just hide them until after a couple of days they found them. After that, they would stand there and watch me take them ☹. I still could not believe they didn't tell me <u>what I was taking</u>. Finally, my mother, father, my Aunt Ida, and friend Yve all went in the doctor's office at different times in one day. They all told him Carolann cannot take these pills and to please tell us what they're for. Finally, they listened and took me off them. Thank God! They were two sleeping pills which I didn't need; I sleep all the time anyway before the pills. A mood tranquilizer; they obviously <u>thought</u> I was in a bad mood because of my injury. They didn't realize then that it was because of their attitudes towards me! They had no personalities. Especially doctors. Thank God we have them. They know a lot and can really help us when we need them. But most of them, especially in hospitals, have no compassion. They don't even know how to have a conversation with you. They treat everyone like they're stupid . . . and they just <u>know everything</u>.

Mynicillin was another drug they were giving me. Well guess what?! If they told me that, I would have told them I AM ALLERGIC TO Mynicillin. I know my body very well and I'm a health fanatic "MACROBIOTIC" . . . that's why I'm so thin!

I've been reading everything possible about it for eight years now. Doctors do not think we can know anything about the body. Obviously they only know about drugs and surgery. They don't know or want to know what you could do to keep yourself healthy.

Well after they stopped feeding me all those pills, my stomach was better and I started to eat again.

It took me about two months to gain my weight back. I was ninety lbs ☹. It is really hard for me to gain weight. I eat too healthy, no meat, no sugar, no salt, no dairy, no alcohol, no bread because I'm allergic to yeast. So it is hard to gain weight if you don't eat some bad things.

I was in Magee Rehabilitation Hospital for five weeks. The therapists there were <u>really good</u>. They made me exercise a little each day and walk a lot. They really got me back into shape. WHAT A DIFFERENCE THAN STAYING IN BED. My body felt so much better ☺!

Before they started doing this, my family and friends helped me so much. The time they spent with me and <u>all</u> their support did so much for me.

A couple of times, cousin Michael would talk to me for so long. He'd let me know how important it was for me to eat. Because if I didn't, I would wilt away to NOTHING . . . I was eating the tiniest bit at that time.

I used to feel so bad for my family. I knew they felt so bad seeing me like this. Even though they tried to hide it from me. But just seeing the there everyday and night, eight to twelve people a day . . . that made me even push myself harder to get out and get home. I could not wait to get back to my normal life with them again.

When I started to eat again, and felt a little better—it was nice to see my family and friends happy again ☺.

That made it easier for me because they would talk about themselves instead of me. It was really getting boring for me. It was really getting boring for me that everything was about me. I would say "how are you?" "what's new?" they'd answer "How are you?" I felt like I didn't know about anyone's life anymore just mine . . . IT WAS SO BORING!!!

One thing I look back a lot though is the spiritual things that happened to me. "THERE IS LIFE AND DEATH" which we all know. Bu there is something afterwards.

I KNOW BECAUSE I WAS THERE!

My memory was lost in the beginning. I did not remember the accident. I just remember my dad coming in my apartment, wanting coffee. He got a cup—came back, we picked up my friend Bianca and my sister Janice and left for New York. Remembered nothing from Newark University Hospital. I didn't remember anyone who had died in my family—prior to my accident!

. . . when I was in Magee Rehab, I would wake up almost everyday and say to one of my family members . . . I just saw Grandmom or one of my uncles. They would just look at me with their eyes opened real wide and say "what did you say?" or "what did they look like?" so finally one day I said to my aunt Louise, "I saw Grandmom last night. Why doesn't she come here with you in the day?" she just stared at me and I saw her eyes watering. Then she said . . . "Carolann, I really think you saw Grandmom and I know she's helping you." Well after that, I started thinking, something's very strange!

So when Tommy came, I said to him, tell me everyone who died in my family. He looked nervous, I said tell I can handle it. I'm making people sad and nervous when I tell them I saw Grandmom or one of my uncles.

So finally he told me . . . Grandmom, Grandpop, Uncle Mike, Uncle Sammy, Uncle Bill, Uncle John, Grandmom, and Grandpop DeBellis.

Each one that he told me about, my heart dropped. Then I remembered right away when he told mea little something about the funeral or how they died. And I felt fine because I remembered mourning over them. I then started telling my family I was just dreaming about them so they wouldn't get nervous about it.

So at that time, I was thinking "I must be dreaming about all these people" . . . but I knew I wasn't dreaming!

. . . I know I saw some of them especially my grandmother. I thought I was dreaming about her EVERY SINGLE DAY. But I know I saw her and she was helping me . . . . Grandmom and I were very close. Every time I would see her she'd hug me and say "Carolann, you better eat. You are going to get sick. Or she'd say "Grandmom (she'd call her grandchildren Grandmom sometimes), please go back and eat your food. You are going to get too thin." Then she'd say, "Promise," and I'd say, "Okay, Grandmom."

I love you

So one day they brought breakfast in and I started to eat for the first time, since I arrived at Magee. This is before they stopped my pills. My doctor walked in and started screaming, "YOU'RE EATING, YOU'RE EATING!"

He called a few nurses and doctors in and they were all saying, "We can't believe it! You're eating!" I looked at them and said "I'm doing it for Grandmom," and I was. ☺

Grandmom definitely helped me and I know I saw her everyday . . . I LOVED BEING WITH HER AGAIN!

Another thing that happened was . . . my Aunt Ida was sleeping in the waiting room in Newark Hospital. One night at 3:00 am, she woke up (I don't remember this, I was unconscious a lot then). She came to my room and held my hand. She said I woke up startled, and said

"Aunt Ida, I was looking for you. I just saw Uncle Bill (he's Aunt Ida's husband who died three years prior)." She said, "Where? How did he look?" I said, "he had khaki pants on and a plaid shirt." "I was going through a long dark tunnel and there was a light at the end of it. When I got to the end, I saw him and got SO EXCITED! I said, 'Uncle Bill, Uncle Bill' with my arms out to hug him. He just looked at me and said, 'Carolann, go on—go on, you're NOT MY DAUGHTER—go-on, go-on.'"

. . . I was so upset that he wouldn't hug me. Uncle Bill and I were so close. I never heard him raise his voice at anyone. Or speak negatively. He was the most pleasant man you'd ever want to meet. I couldn't believe he wasn't excited to see me.

So Aunt Ida said after I told her all this I fell back to sleep. My poor aunt just stood there in shock for about twenty minutes. She couldn't move. She knew I saw him—I would never say "go-on go-on" he was from Texas, that's how he spoke. I would have said "get out of here."

She prayed to Uncle Bill a lot. That night she said, "Please, Bill if you see Carolann, send her back. She's NOT READY TO COME THERE! PLEASE SEND HER BACK!"
. . . and **he did.**

First, here's my schedule I had to do Monday through Friday . . .

Grandmom Giulietta with her twin brother Romero (Romeo
and Juliet)

Grandmom with Daughters . . .
Aunt Louise, Aunt Toni, and Aunt Jean

Aunt Ida and Uncle Bill on their Wedding Day
April 27, 1957

Uncle Bill and Aunt Ida with their children Bill and Michelle.
Sandy and Michelle with their children Chessa and Ali.

THERAPY SCHEDULE

I feel like this was the hardest thing I've ever done in my life—worse than school . . . I hated school.

	Time	Place	Therapist
Monday	10:15-10:45	OT	Joann
	10:45-11:15	ST	Sylvia
	11:15-11:45	PT	Nancy
	1:15-1:45	RT	Rena
	2:15-2:45	OT	Joanne
	2:45-3:45	PT	Nancy
Tuesday	10:15-10:45	OT	Joann
	10:45-11:15	ST	Sylvia
	11:15-11:45	PT	Nancy
	2:15-2:45	OT	Joanne
	2:45-3:45	PT	Nancy
	4:00-4:45	Rec Gr.	Rena
Wednesday	10:15-10:45	OT	Joann
	10:45-11:15	ST	Sylvia

	11:15-11:45	OT	Nancy
	1:15-1:45	RT	Rena
	2:15-2:45	OT	Joann
	2:45-3:45	PT	Kellie
Thursday	9:00-9:45	Neuropsych	Joanne
	10:15-10:45	OT	Joanne
	10:45-11:15	ST	Sylvia
	11:15-11:45	PT	Nancy
	2:15-2:45	OT	Joann
	2:45-3:45	PT	Nancy
Friday	9:00-9:45	Music	Rena
	10:15-10:45	OT	Joann
	10:45-11:15	ST	Sylvia
	11:15-11:45	PT	Nancy
	2:15-2:45	OT	Joann
	2:45-3:45	PT	Nancy

Here are some notes people wrote when they come in my room at Magee . . .

2/13/87

Speech Therapy—
Carol had complaints of being sick and made frequent requests to go to the bathroom. She was capable of verbalizing some biographical information accurately and calmed down slightly when moved around in hallway.

Speech Affiliate

PT—this afternoon in PT, we worked on Carol's evaluation from 2:45-3:45.

Nancy

OT—This morning, Carol was very focused on being cold, nauseous, and sleepy. She told me about her work, aerobics, and nautilus. We attempted to do manual muscle tests of her arms, but she did not give any resistance during the test; I will try again during Monday therapy. In the afternoon, I tested active movement of her arms, and there doesn't seem to be any limitations in her joints.

Joanne Staymajh

2/13/87

Visitors
Tom, Daddy, Renee, Janice, Aunt Ida and Aunt Louse, and Michelle, and Mari.

2/13/87

Tom (Husband) and Janice and Renee (sisters) tried repeatedly to get Carol to eat. She managed to take liquids, but refused food. At 6:30 she asked to go to the bathroom, we took her to the toilet and she had a bowel movement. We tried again to get her to eat, but no success. Janice brought an excellent conditioner/relaxer to use on carol's hair after it is washed. It should remove the tangles in her hair.

7:40 second bowel movement on toilet.

2/14/87

Aunt Ida, Aunt Tony, Mom & Dad DelColle and Tommy visiting today from 2:00. Carolann is awake, alert and as close to her normal self as we have seen since the accident. She ate one full bowl of chicken soup that her aunt brought. She also ate some cut up carrots and celery and drank one cup of chamomile tea, two cups of water, and one cup of orange juice. She sat up on the side of the bed for about ten minutes.

Carolann has expressed a desire for the nursing staff to let her know <u>ahead of time</u> when they will be doing something (shower, rehab, etc).

2/14/87 pm

Carol was very alert this evening as well. She drank liquids frequently.

Carol was able to converse with her visitors; Joan, Vince, Daddy, Frankie and Renee, and Tommy.

2/15/87

Visitors: Tom, Lorraine, Laura, Janice and Renee, Daddy, Fred, Margaret, Christopher, and Mari.

Carol is awake, alert and requested a massage and her vitamins.

4:15 Visitors: Fred, Margaret, and Chris Fred told Carol he saw Rudy. She said they were going to see the play on Tuesday . . . did not mention accident, she also asked where her brother was and Fred said he went to NY overnight. She asked if he saw the play. Fred said no, but it will play again.

She asked if we went to dinner yet, and where we went.

She asked Janice for a massage.

She said Rudy visited the shop a couple of days ago.

2/15/87

Question to Doctor Horn.
Is the anxiety Carollann experiences when she is in an upright position a common symptom?

Tom

Would it be ok for us to have a masseuse come to the hospital?

Tom

This evening Carol ate with no resistance a bowl of cabbage and most of a bowl of spinach as well as noodles.

2/16/87

Occupational Therapy
I attempted to do "strength test" of your arms. Overall, your shoulders were weaker than your elbow and wrist muscles.

Joanne

2/16/87

Speech
Carol did not make as many complaints today, but still became restless after 10-15 minutes. Change of setting (moving around in hallway) offered some calming effect for her. Answers to questions were at time exaggerated but most were appropriately answered. Also stated that she has "bad memory now" and can't remember things.

Pat Staton

2/16/87 2:15

OC
This afternoon, she continued to complain about feeling nauseous and cold. She laid on the mat and answered some questions about orientation she was so oriented to herself, place, and time.

Joanne

2/16/87

Carolann did well today. She is more compliant when allowed to do tasks at her own pace. She has attended all of her therapies today. Carolann has spent most of her free time in the television room on the couch. Carolann has also been eating better when set up in the television room. Therefore, feedings will continue in the television room and continue to be evaluated on a daily basis. PT will first be brought into dining room with other PT's. Depending on distractions, pt will be brought into the t.v. room.

Lisa Yedman RN

2/16/87

Physical   Therapy
Carol attended PT for thirty minutes in the am and sixty minutes in the pm. She continues to complain of dizziness and nausea especially when sitting, but she was much more compliant today. We worked on a lot of leg exercises for strengthening. Carol's right leg is weaker than the let. We also worked on sitting balance and sitting tolerance while Carol was sitting on the edge of the mat. Carol also worked on standing, and she even took about four steps with assistance.

I got Carol a new wheelchair which will hopefully be more comfortable for her.

Nancy

2/16

I am Carol's Aunt Ida from Texas. I was in Newark, NJ with Carol for two weeks before she was transferred to Magee. The change in her since I first saw her has been unbelievable. I feel she is on her way and once her head is cleared and she realizes everything that is going on, she will work very hard to get her body back in good physical condition. Please be patient, she is a very special young lady.

Some of my cousins
Fred, Sharon, Julie's Birthday

2/16

carol had dinner tonight at 5:00. she ate fish, lima beans, and baked potatoes. She ate with no resistance. As soon as she finished, she wanted to get back into bed.

Tommy

At 7:00 carol went for a walk with her family for about 15 minutes. While in her chair she remained in good spirits and seemed to enjoy the walk. It was an effort to get her in the chair though, but not as difficult as before. This was the first I saw Carol sit without sliding and complaining. We used the chair without the bar.

Renee

2/16/87

visitors: Tom, Aunt Ida, Aunt Louise, Daddy, Janice, and Renee.

2/17/87

Physical Therapy
This morning we worked on Carol's sitting balance without the support of her chair. She also did all of her leg strengthening exercises. She seems to be tolerating sitting in the chair a lot better.

This afternoon Carol stood at the parallel bars twice for about thirty seconds. Then she walked the length of the parallel bars and back to her chair (about 15-20 feet). After that, Carol got on the mat and I stretched out her legs. She was _very_ tired. We played TicTacToe, and then a memory game while she rested.

Carol wheeled her own wheelchair back to her room form therapy—please encourage her to wheel herself as much as possible. She need only a little assistance for steering.

Nancy

2/17/87

Occupational Therapy
Carol was somewhat agitated today as she needed to go to the bathroom several times during the session. She was able to sit in the wheelchair the full half hour this afternoon.

Joanne

Carolann's visitors that came today were Aunt Louse, Uncle Dante, Aunt Ida, Mommy, Little Rudy, Janice, Renee, Daddy, Tommy, Denise, and Aunt Rita.

Carol ate a full bowl of okra, an entire potato and some beans.

She wheeled herself to the hallway, went to the bathroom, came back to her room about twenty minutes later and wanted to get back into bed immediately.

Carol stayed awake a lot later than usual.

2/18/87 9:15 am

Carol had a hard time with breakfast and tried very hard not to go to PT. She said that she honestly had a headache.

Tom

2/18/87 10:45 am

This morning, I worked on dressing with Carol. She got up at 8:30. she put her pants and underwear on rather quickly, and started to put them on backwards. She sat on the edge of the bed to put her sweatshirt on. She needed some help as her sitting balance isn't the best. She tends to fall backwards easily.

In therapy, we did a clinical eye test. She did not appear to have any problems except her acuity was decreased. Carol told me she used glasses to read.

Joanne

2/18/87

Wednesday
OT
Once Carol got out of bed and focused on the activity, she did not complain as much about being sick.

This afternoon we did a sensory test for arms, testing cold, hot sharp/dull, and naming objects in her hand by sense of feel. She did well in this test. No problems.

Joanne

2/18/87

Physical Therapy
This morning in PT, Carol worked on her unsupported sitting balance, and then worked on her leg strengthening exercises. This afternoon we spent a lot of time on Carol's seating since she is so uncomfortable sitting in a wheelchair. I got her a reclining wheelchair with a high back—I need to make some adjustments and will have it ready tomorrow. We also did more exercises, and then Carol walked the length of the parallel bars twice.

Nancy

2/18/87

Dinnertime: Carol ate all of her vegetables (zucchini) a little turkey, and chicken soup with noodles, turnips, carrots, and chicken (homemade by Dan from NYC) one cup.

2/18/87

I thought Carol was great. Very talkative and a lot of fun. Remembered everything about me and Anthony and ate well.

Cousin Sharon

2/18/87

Carol drank two cups of water with dinner. She wheeled herself to the sixth floor and around for about fifteen minutes. She also walked to the bathroom with assistance.

2/19/87

Occupational Therapy
Carol spent seventeen minutes of her therapy in her wheelchair without too many complaints about being dizzy. We continued to do some more of the cognitive assessment. Carol usually knows the day and the month, but at times, she is confused about what time it is (morning or afternoon). We talked about how she just ate breakfast and didn't have lunch yet to alert her to the time of day. She remembered she had an omelet for breakfast.

I asked her some simple math problems. She did good with addition and subtraction but had some trouble with remembering multiplication and division. But at the time, she seemed more focused on her dizziness, so she may not have been able to concentrate.

Joanne

2/19/87

Speech Therapy
Carolann had half of speech session in therapy room and half of session in her room. She was able to direct therapist to her room and talked about her tea, she uses for soothing her stomach. She consistently gave appropriate responses to questions asked.

Pat Stator, Graduate Affiliate

2/19/87

Physical Therapy
This morning Carol was late for PT because she was still eating her breakfast. She got on the mat and did some of her leg exercises.

This afternoon we spent most of her PT session working on her seating and getting her in a chair that will be more comfortable for her. She did not feel any more comfortable in the reclining chair. I will try to get her a different one tomorrow.

Nancy

2/19/87

Carol was eating dinner when Gina and I arrived. She ate carrots and Aunt Ida kept sneaking chicken in with the carrots, but she was awake and <u>funny</u>. She complained about being nauseous, but that was about all. She said she would play bingo on Saturday with me and she also wanted to talk to Aunt Annie.

Anthony

2/20/87 10:45

Occupational therapy
This morning we finished a perception test I had started with Carol yesterday. Perception is our brain's ability to visually analyze what we see in our environment.

She sat in the w/c (wheelchair) for about twelve minutes. I used the timer and that seems to help her tolerate staying in the chair longer. Although she did complain about being sick, she complained much less this morning.

Joanne

2/20/87

OT
This afternoon, Carol stayed in her w/c for fifteen minutes. She then go out of the chair and sat on the edge of the mat for ten minutes. She lay down after this. We played tic-tac-toe with cones while she worked on her short sitting balance (feet on floor).

Joanne

2/20/87

Physical Therapy
I gave Carol a reclining wheelchair today, and she says she feels too sick to be able to tell if it's any better than her other chair. She looks better in the reclining chair. Tom, let me know what you think since you'll probably spend the most time with her while she's in the chair. I'm hoping that she'll be more comfortable, and be able to sit up for longer. Thanks

Nancy

2/20/87

An Observation
By Tom DelColle

As the days go on, I begin to see a patter in CarolAnn's behavior. What makes this pattern apparent to me is that it is the same way that she acted before the accident, only intensified. For instance, we find CarolAnn to be very moody and uncooperative in the morning. This is probably because she has never been "a morning person." She takes a long time in the morning to get up and into her routine, about an hour.

As far as her complaining about nausea, backache, leg pains, etc, I believe that Carol can exaggerate a small ailment to make it work to her advantage. After some conversation with Carol, I can feel sure in saying that the one complaint that is truly valid is nausea and upset stomach. This contributes greatly to the problem we have with her eating. I bring this to your attention so that we may be able to help her resolve this problem. (Please show this to Dr. Horn).

Thank you

Cousin Anthony who dances VERY WELL!
. . . his sister Michele to the left . . .

Cousin Michele, also a GOOD DANCER with Me
. . . Uncle Sammy & Aunt Carol in back ☺

2/20/87

Carol seems to be more aggravated than yesterday. Tonight, we put her in the reclining wheelchair and she was able to sit up longer.

2/21/87

Tonight, Carol walked to the bathroom and had a bowel movement.

2/22/87

Carol was up in her chair for an hour and a half; Aunt Ida and Aunt Toni were here. Carol walked to the bathroom by herself twice. Said she'd eat in the dining room today. Rudy, Margaret, Christopher, Bianca, Renee, Bella were here; Tommy and his Mom.

2/22/87

Carol ate very well at lunch and dinner today. We did not make an issue out of her eating, it seems to have worked. Carol said she was looking forward to PT tomorrow and said she felt more tired because of no exercise.

2/22/87

Visitors today—later—Debbie and Michael and Dan. Carol is very calm and awake and talkative. She walked several times assisted by Tommy—a few steps across the room to Michael and then back and then again for her dad. Also to the bathroom and back. Cousin Michael massaged Carol's back.

Carol seems sincerely interested in getting out of the hospital and knows she'll need to walk and eat better to get out. The various pills she's taking are upsetting her stomach and making her feel nauseous.

She also complains about being forced to take a shower at 11 pm last night. She says she's tired but seems very awake to me—I guess she longs for her full energy. Despite all the complaints, Carol has a great sense of humor and is extremely sociable.

Dan

2/23/87

Recreation—I met with CarolAnn for the first time today. Although we were able to have a pleasant discussion (and discuss her past interests and lifestyle), CarolAnn did complain of nausea, aches, eating, dismay, etc., and did say that she had an ambition to participate in recreation activities but didn't have the "physical" desire. I told her that we would take things slowly but that I would encourage her and possibly push her in some activities/participation. CarolAnn was compliant.

Rena

2/23/87

OT

Today, CarolAnn seemed much less agitated than usual. Outside, some of her usual complaints, Carol worked on the armbike and did 100 revolutions without complaining. She then stood up for approximately three minutes while she did math calculations. Carol worked intently and expressed wanting to get better soon. She is anxious to begin exercising again. Carol was a pleasure to work with.

Jim (covering for Joanne today).

2/23/87

Physical Therapy
Carol is like a new person today—she's all smiles, and hardly complains at all! She was very cooperative, and did a lot of work. She

did all her leg exercises, worked on sitting and standing balance, and walking. She really had a good day with me!

Nancy

Tom—I would be glad to show you Carol's exercises—she said she'd like to do them at night and on weekends

Nancy

Feb. 23, 1987

"Carol Barrell"—was terrific today! Pauline says so! Yve and Bianca came with me. It was wonderful to see her. Her spirits were wonderful but she expresses a big, fat desire to get the "hell out of this place!" good sign—we love you, sweetheart—hurry home!!!

Pauline, Bianca, & Yve

Carol ate all her dinner with the exception of the soup—but I brought about six ounces of pasta and beans (she likes this) and she ate all of it.

Ida Ray

I'd like to add that I fed Carol (with little resistance) slowly but surely, she reached the goal. Alleluia!

Cousin Rachael

Feb. 24, 1987

OT
Copied lines and dots.

This morning, Carol did some standing with help for about two minutes. She tends to lean more on the left. We then got out of the wheelchair and she sat in a regular chair without any problems.

In the afternoon, she did a perception test (copying lines and dots). It is a test to see if what Carol is seeing, her brain is interpreting correctly.

Joanne

2/24/87

Physical Therapy
Today, Carol did lots of walking for short distances with minimal assistance. We tried the rolling walker, but she walks better without. She also did a lot of stretching and strengthening exercises, and worked on balancing. She's improving a lot!

Nancy

2/24/87

Today, Carol was much less annoyed in the morning. Breakfast went down easy. She was very cooperative throughout the day. We spoke on the phone twice. For dinner, she ate everything on the tray plus soup that her aunt brought. We are all very excited about her progress.

Tommy

2/25/87

Recreation
Doing different and new things (make-up) filing nails, swimming, facial, thank you notes!
    Tom—please bring in hand cream make-up.

Rena

2/25/87

dressed myself
OT
High-Q-cups

Work on standing
Arm bicycle
Bending-cards

Today, Carol dressed herself, brushed her hair and teeth herself.

In the morning, we worked on her standing tolerance and balance. She stood about ten minutes. We played a game called HiQ while she stood so she would not hold on with her hands while she stood.

This afternoon, she did 150 repetitions on the arm bike while standing. We also sat on the edge of the mat and bent down to a low table to play cards. She did not get dizzy at all.

Joanne

2/25/87

Physical Therapy
This morning, Carol walked with minimal assistance around the PT gym. She also did some leg and stomach exercises.

This afternoon, Carol walked again, and then we worked in the parallel bars for strengthening, balancing and improving the way she walks. Then Carol rode the exercise bike for one mile. She finished up doing some more leg exercises.

What a surprise! I was so happy to see Carol, looking better than I imagined. Of course, I'm used to her speaking much louder. She's gonna be yelling at me again in no time. Squeeze, squeeze, left, right. I believe she's come a long way and maybe she has a long way to go, but seeing her gives me confidence that she will be much stronger than ever before. Do it, Carol.

Love you,
Cynthia

2/26/87

OT
Do the arm bike till 152. was fun. Play High Q. left 3 cup to work on legs and strengthening.

Bat over to get 1 cup for water (3rd drawer).

2/26/87

Occupational Therapy
This morning, carol dressed herself while sitting in bed. She put on her sneakers but it was a little hard.

In the morning, Tom came to therapy with Carol. While standing, Carol did 150 repetitions on the eigonmenter (arm bike).

With assistance, from standing she bent down to get a cup from a low drawer.

This afternoon, we did some perceptual tasks of copying designs with blocks, where Carol had to judge various angles. She did much better with this activity than she did last week. We also played Boggle, to work on her writing.

Joanne

2/27/87

My name is Kettha. I'm a student nurse in my senior year working with Carol. I was here last Thursday and Friday, and this Thursday and Friday. I will also be here next Thursday and Friday. Today, Carol ate in the dining room with the rest of the patients on the floor. She ate all of her breakfast and most of her lunch. She had a lot more energy today than yesterday.

2/27/87

CarolAnne has been terrific today; a real chance since last week. CarolAnne has been initiating more (hunger, bathroom, etc.) CarolAnne ate all of her meals in the dining room with everyone else and ate well. I will be back tomorrow evening at 3 pm. See you.

Lisa (3-11 nurse)

2/27/87

Physical Therapy
This morning, Carol did some walking around the halls with littleassistance, and she rode the exercise bike for one mile.

This afternoon we did some more walking. Then we worked at the parallel bars and concentrated on control of Carol's walking. She sat on the big green ball and worked on balancing and bouncing. She and I also did a lot of leg and trunk exercises. Next week carol will begin in exercise class at 3:15 everyday. She's really improving fast!

Nancy

2/27/87

today was the first day I didn't come to see CarolAnn for breakfast. I called her early to see if she was ok . . . she sounded great and was very positive. Tonight when I arrived, she seemed more herself than I've seen. I'm real happy with her progress.

Tommy

Today I came to see carol. Yet! It's Carol alright. She's the best I've seen her yet. But then again, I am a Friday night visitor.

Love you, Carol
Keep on, Keep on,
Frankie (not bad)

3/1/87

1. Breakfast 8:00-8:30 Dining Room
2. Go to room, get pills, and pass to go home
3. Dress, clothes on top shelf—with sneakers
4. Must be back before 8:00 pm
5. Pills up to 6:00 pm

2/28

I haven't been to see Carol for a few days and can't believe the progress she's made since my last visit. I really notice a change. I was so surprised—she is talking much, much more and very awake.

3/2

I will forever remember Carol as a miracle happening before my eyes. With her strong will, sense of self, and the unselfish love of others, she has been making a remarkable recovery. I enjoy getting to know Carol with each visit with her. I hope that she will write her book for others to share in her wisdom.

Tommy, thanks for including me, as I have had a need to give.

Carol, I am so happy you are smiling. I am sure the staff at Magee is pleased with your progress and will benefit from getting to know you.

God bless you.

3/4

I haven't written in this book for a week or so, because now Carol has so much to say—I haven't had the chance. She is doing terrific. Carol is more herself than ever. Eating well, smiling, giving advice and best of all, doing for herself (her hair, brushing her teeth, make-up, etc.).

she calls me over the phone and tells me an account of her day (Carol always did this). I am so happy.

Renee

3/4

Our CarolAnn is just doing great—really a pleasure to be with—she's very happy.

Aunt Louise

Me, Tom, Brother-in-law Frankie,
Sister Renee's husband
1984

3/5/87

Speech
We have almost completed Carol's evaluation. Right now, we're testing how she does on everyday activities such as telephone skills, money management, etc. I also made a consult to the ENT (ear, nose and throat) doctor to make sure Carol's vocal cords are intact. I have noticed her hoarseness and want to doublecheck as a precaution. Will let you know of the results.

Sylvia

3/5/87

Visitors: Mom and Dad DelColle and Laina

3/6/87

Carol was alert and <u>talkative!!</u> She seems to be back to normal with few exceptions. Aunt Louise, Aunt Jean, Uncle Frank—Janice, Jeff, Francis, and Sonny visited today.

3/7/87

Carol is very excited today. We're going home and we'll spend some time in the sunshine. She'll be back this evening with Tom and back home tomorrow.

Renee

March 9-87 6:20 pm

Oh well, another day—Janice made me very nervous. She just would not get off the chair.

Lucy

3/9/87

Yesterday (3/8/87) carol was home for the day. She cut her bangs and did a terrific job. She ate well and was in good spirits.

Renee

3/10/87

Speech
Result of assessments were explained to CarolAnn. She was told about her verbosity, grammatural deficits, and deficits for insight concerning her problem.

State Student Affiliate

3/10/87

carol seems to be more aware of the total situation (physical, mental, emotional). According to her, home is not too far away. Just a little more physical therapy.

3/12/87

Speech Therapy
CarolAnn interpreted short stories read to her. She was able to take a phone message and convey it back with minimal errors (she left out the location). After completing this task, she was able to answer adequately questions presented to her about the two previous short stories discussed. We had a good session, Carol!

Pat Stator
Grad Affiliate

3/12/87

Physical Therapy
Today Carol worked on jumping and balancing activities. She also rode the bike, and did the rowing machine for endurance. She and I walked down to the second floor, and Carol practiced getting in a nd out of the bathtub. She did very well.

Carol's main physical problems are her balance, and her ability to jump, but she's improving with practice.

Nancy

3/13/87

Speech
CarolAnn is using shorter verbalizations to response to info from short stories presented to her. She also related information that was in her log book.

P Stator

3/16/87

Speech
Reading paragraphs for sequencing events. Retelling info from paragraphs. Discussion and recall of newspaper article on haircolor, wigs, and styling.

Pat Stator

Memo's
Rena 3/18 6:30-7:00 swimming
"Wed" 1:00
Tom, bring in Louie bag of
Double sessions cape
Spray bottle
Blow dryer
Bathing suit
Swimming
Rena

3/16/87

I'm really starting to feel like myself now. Everyday I feel better and better.

I really thank the therapists and nurses a lot for this, they really care and work their hardest to help people here.

I've always liked and tried my hardest to help people in my life. It really makes me want to come back to this hospital when I get out, and help patients, maybe in exercise or something.

Carol

3/17/87

Speech
Went over notes CarolAnn put in log book.

Discussed yesterday's activities in therapies. Successfully able to decrease verbosity when requested to do so.

Carol was able to recall inform. from paragraphs and give me sentence conclusion for each.

Pat Stator

3/17

OT (What I did)
In OT, I rode the bike for 10 mins. Stretch machine for 5 mins. Sit ups-15X, bridging—15X, side leg—15X (both sides), straight leg raise (15X) stomach, bend knees—15X, lift legs strength—15X.

Coming up: hair cut Wed 3/18 1:00
Perm & haircut Friday 3/20 12:30

3/17

Had a real nice day today. I had a lot of therapies, and I feel very good from them.

Carol

Carol looked great, I was really excited. We all came to visit Sharon, Aunt Jill, Uncle Buster, Aunt Louise, Renee, and Martin. Went with her for dinner and talked like always. Always make me feel good. I love you, Cousin.

Love, Sharon XO

3/18

Today was really nice; a few more therapies were put in my day, a meeting with my social worker, and necro-psychology. Also, I did a haircut <u>standing up</u> (which was exciting).

3/20/87

Speech
CarolAnn—Thank you so much for the lovely flowers. I was really surprised but appreciate your thoughtfulness and kindness.

Pat Stator

Fri
I had such a wonderful day today. I did a perm and haircut and conducted an exercise class. I really felt great doing all that.

I also said goodbye to Pat, she's a really nice person. I'll miss her.

Carol

Dear Carol,   3·11·87

After one of our visits I stopped
off to have an apple juice inside
the cap there was a message —
"Tears are summer showers
    to the soul."
Keep laughing and crying and
talking and feeling and
searching for that truly
wonderful person you are!
Each process you put yourself
through, only helps you to
understand, more and more,
who you are. ———— it's fantastic.
These past few months have taught me so much
more about myself. Thank you for helping me feel
the essence of unconditional love.
                    Love, Cousin Michael

(4th floor)

Carol Del Colle
Magee Rehabilitation
    Hospital
6 Franklin Plaza
Phila. Pa

Michael writing beautiful card while I was in "Magee Rehab"

MONDAY: VERY DEFINITE NEWS!

HOMEWARD BOUND THURSDAY!!
GREAT WORK MAGEE AND CAROLANN

TOM TOO, OF COURSE

SHE'S GOING HOME—

YAHOO!

HOORAY!

YIPPEE!

"HAPPY DAY!"

3/24

PHYSICAL THERAPY

I AM BEGINNING TO DEVELOP A HOME PROGRAM
FOR CAROL. HER PRIMARY DEFICITS ARE HIGH-
LEVEL BALANCE ACTIVITIES SUCH AS JUMPING,
RUNNING, QUICKLY CHANGING DIRECTIONS
AND WALKING ON THE BALANCE BEAM.

GERI

THURSDAY, MARCH 26,

1987

GOING HOME

YEAH!!!

Renee, Mommy, Me and Tommy

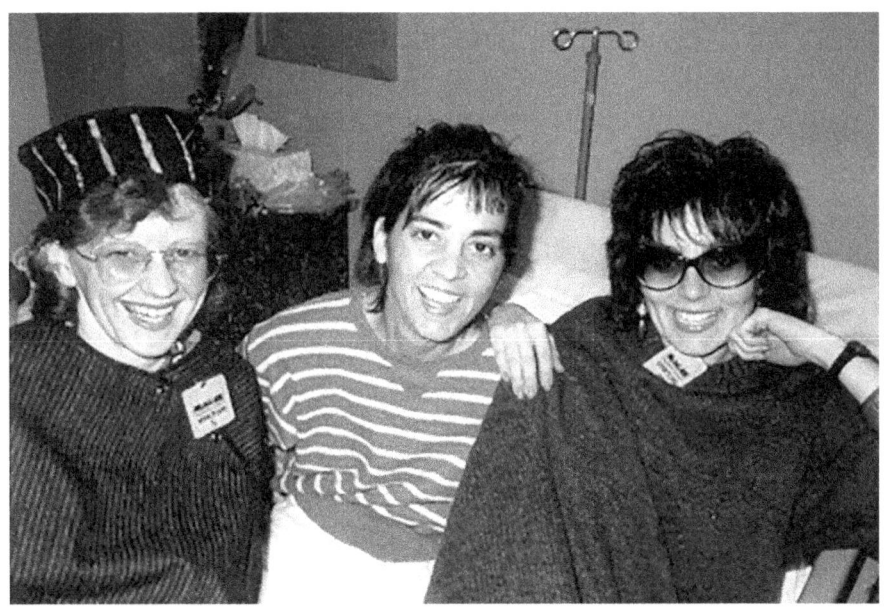

Mari (good friend who donated time at Magee)
Me & Renee

Tommy, Renee & Me
(I was down to 90 lbs.) ☹

Renee, Janice, Cindy (friend I worked with
at Pileggi's), Me and Tommy

Carol,

From the beginning —
even while in aun unconscious
state — you taught me.
... I again learn from you.

Get Well Soon!
I love you kis —
you are very special
to me.

Renée

A Caring & Beautiful Note from Renee

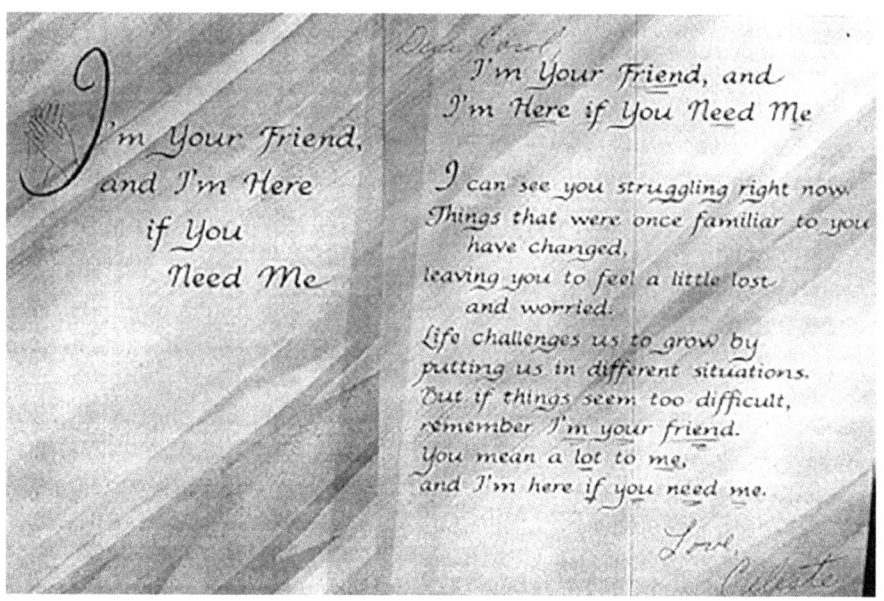

Another Beautiful Caring Card from my good friend Celeste

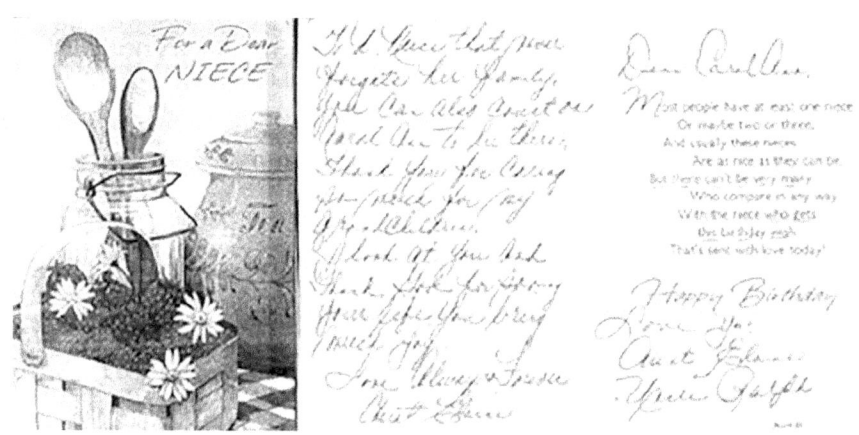

My dear Aunt Elaine & Uncle Ralph for my Birthday
April 17th

I know that no matter what happens to you in life—it is meant to happen. If someone dies in an accident, people say, "he shouldn't have gone there today. If they stayed home, they would still be alive." That is not true . . . I believe it was that person's time.

I had a friend, Meg's twin brother, Jim Henninger that used to live in Avon, Connecticut. His family moved to California. One year later, Jim died. He went fishing with his dad and drowned. I used to say, "If Jim didn't move, he'd still be here with us." But I don't believe that anymore. When we are meant to die, we die.

"A time to be born"

"A time to die"

. . . Jim sang and danced with me to this song when I was 13.

"Turn, turn, turn"

. . . When Jim drowned, his father unfortunately watched and couldn't do a thing. Jim was standing across the river from his dad. Mr. Henninger said "Don't go into the water, Jim, it's rough underneath!"

. . . Jim answered, "I lost my 'lure' I have to"—then his "waders" filled up with water and he went under. His dad was so far away, he couldn't get to him ☹ . . . the only thing that helped his dad not to lose it completely was . . . He is very close to God—He has faith, and he believes . . .

Are you ready for this?

Mr. Henninger actually saw an image of a "white dove" come down from the sky, go to the water, and then two images of "two white doves" came from the water, going all the way up to the sky . . . knowing that he went to heaven. At <u>the same time</u>, Meg, Jim's sister, was sitting miles away in front of a lake with her fiance. She said to her fiance, "I just felt Jim all around me"—she actually turned around thinking he was there. It was so strong. Before her brother Jim had left that morning, he hugged her, kissed her and said "I love you, Meg" something he <u>rarely did.</u>

We know when we die there's no more body. We wilt away to nothing. Just our soul and inner self survives. When I saw my grandmother and my Uncle Bill, everyone asked "How did they look?" Grandmom was dressed in a flowered dress. That's how she dressed everyday. Uncle Bill had on khaki pants with a red and blue plaid shirt—that's how he dressed.

God presented them that way to me. Because that's how I remembered them. If I just heard their voices, I would not have thought I had seen them!

After reuniting with Meg 30 years later, I learned she had almost lost her first born son in a drowning accident. I thought, "Oh my God, she lost her twin brother and now I am learning she almost lost her first born son too". He had been spear fishing off the coast of Fiji at just 17 years of age. He was swept out to sea and spent the entire night in the ocean. Many times he sank down and was about to drown but he said he felt the presence of angels lifting him out of the water. He ended up landing on another island many miles away and surviving the jungle to finally be rescued. It is an incredible and miraculous story that leads to his survival. The point being, Jesse was not suppose to die yet!!

. . . Because he now has a beautiful wife, Maria and two beautiful children, Jahleel and Hallei.

Me with Mr. Henninger No
picture of Jim ☹

Sandy, Editor of my book ☺
Me, Husband of Michelle, Cousin Michelle, Meg, Meg's Sister Lisa

When I first came home from the hospital, I was so happy and so ready to get back to my life. I stayed home for a month until I got some of my energy back. I'm a hairstylist, I stand up and don't stop all day, so I definitely needed energy. The doctor told me I should take it easy for about six months to a <u>year.</u> They told my husband I may never work again and I may not remember who he is at times. My husband was a nervous wreck that month. He always stared at me in a strange way and he would call me about 4-5 times a day to see how I was doing. All I did was sit and write, read or try and exercise a bit to get my energy back. After a week went by, I asked Tommy, "why are you staring at me like that?" Finally, after much pushing, he told me what the doctors had said. Poor thing, he went through <u>so much.</u> When I was in the coma, they'd pass the room and say "how you doing, buddy?" he'd look up and say, "I don't know." They'd say, "I don't know if she's going to make it." And they would just walk away. How ignorant!

I had to prove to myself, to my family, and to my doctors and nurses that I could live the way I used to.

I was an "out patient" at Magee three times a week. Learning to walk better, teaching me to cook, and they let me cut the doctor—and nurse staff's hair.

I was seeing a "brain injury counselor" named Rhona Cohen. She told me I wasn't mentally ready to cut hair. Even though I still gave a good haircut. They said my tolerance level wasn't ready to deal with people. My doctor Lawrence Horn was an excellent doctor; he knew what he talked about. He was the first one who let me cut his hair . . . God bless him—he had no idea what was going to happen. He was happy with my haircut. But also said you're not ready! Physically or mentally.

I am HEADSTRONG! I never listened to anyone. Always thought I was right. Usually found out I was wrong after all.

Well, after a month of out-patient therapies, I went back to work.

I was out of work for four months. So I lost 75% of my clientele. They got used to other stylists and stayed with them when I came back. That hurt my ego. I went from making tons of money per week To $200. per week. Also, I couldn't handle fulltime work. I worked three days for four hours a day. Came home, cooked dinner, shopped once a week, and did everything like before. No one could believe how I was doing! They were shocked! Especially my doctors. I felt FANTASTIC!!

I obviously pushed myself too hard! After about four months, it hit me. I felt like I just got hom from the hospital—even worse! I was so tired. It was hard to deal with <u>anything</u>. And I HATED EVERYTHING!

I HATED WORK—I HATED COOKING—I HATED SHOPPING —I HATED WHERE I LIVED—I HATED LIFE! ☹

I didn't like myself anymore. I used to be a very pleasant person. I loved life!! I loved people! I was always a person who loved to help people with their problems and everything. At that time, I didn't care about people anymore.

For instance, when my friend Debbie Moffo of 36 years would call just to talk about her problems or whatever—I had no patience! I would cut her short or say really mean things to her. If she was telling me about a situation she was in, I would just break in at times and say "that was really stupid, Debbie, I have to go. Bye" and I'd hang up. Sometimes she would call my husband and just cry to him. Sorry I did that to you Debbie ☹.

I was not Carol, she didn't understand! . . . of course she didn't understand—the Carol in the past would have listened for an hour or more. Then try to make her feel better. Or I'd try to make it funny.

Friends would call me if they had a problem and needed to talk 1-2-3 o'clock in the morning, and I would NEVER get mad. I would love to listen and try to help them. I loved helping people WHENEVER IT MAY HAVE BEEN.

People used to tell me I should be a therapist because I was always helping people and LOVING IT! ☹ I never thought of changing my career for one minute because being a hairstylist is like being a therapist. Some clients would cry in my chair. Especially when you got to know them well; pampering and touching them really made them open up. I learned to go by the client. If they are quiet, they just want to be pampered. If they talk and open up, I would talk and open up . . . they are paying for my service so I got by what they want!

I also have another close friend, Joseph Greco, who worked at Pileggi's for seven years. He was being his normal self, kidding around with me, etc. I was so unfriendly and sarcastic ALL THE TIME. I obviously had no sense of humor anymore. It took about two years to get that back again.

One main thing I forgot after my brain injury was feelings.

My husband used to say at times . . .

"How's Joseph—how's Debbie—how's Bianca, etc." "We never see them anymore," he'd ask. I would answer "Why should we see them, I see them at work." I talk to Debbie on the phone once in a while," I said. "Carol," he would say, "you were so close to them. You used to talk on the phone with Debbie almost every night for half an hour or so. And Joseph used to come over here every Thursday with Mark for dinner. Tippy's Taco's, we had every Thursday night," he said. I was shocked— I didn't remember this <u>at all</u>!

I remember we were friends because I remember knowing them **PHYSICALLY**. Then I would say, "I don't remember feeling LOVE for them." Then I would say, "they changed, I don't like them as much as I used to . . . I guess?!"

It's so strange as I look back, I actually thought everybody changed. Not realizing—**IT WAS ME WHO HAD CHANGED!** Then it hit me. One night, Tommy and I were watching a movie about a couple. The husband was getting upset because the wife was doing <u>too much</u>. He was afraid she would hurt herself. But he didn't tell her; he jut held it in, like Tommy does. I said, "Tommy, they remind me of us, "and he ask why. Well, I went on for about AN HOUR talking about how I realized that I'm pushing myself too hard and you wouldn't dare tell me. Because you know I wouldn't listen anyway and how mad I would get at you. I said, "I am so mean to everyone—I say whatever is on my mind." I tell Debbie she's stupid. I cut her short all the time."

I'm mean to Joseph—he teases me about leaving so early from work. I tell him to mind his own business.

I feel like I'm a child and I didn't learn manners yet. I say anything I feel without thinking first. I NEED TO LEARN TO BE POLITE! I went on and on and as I was telling him, he had tears in his eyes and said, "I KNOW, CAROL! I answered, "Why didn't you tell me?" "I couldn't," he said, "you would have left me or asked me to leave. I wanted you to find out for yourself," and I did, THANK GOD!

I know I would have asked him to leave thinking HE had changed and NOT ME.

Tommy hugged me and cried.

Me and Debbie
1989

Joseph, Mark, Tommy, Joan Pileggi (Boss
& Friend of Pileggi's) and Me
1985

Me & Bianca
"Campbell Soup Kids"
We always got dressed Halloween at Work ☺
1985

<u>I WAS SO HAPPY</u> I BECAME AWARE OF THIS!! ☺ Then I realized what this all boiled down to was . . . I didn't love myself anymore.

It's funny how everything I said to him that night was actually the very first time I ever thought about that consciously. It's like bricks came down and woke my brain up.

You have to love yourself first, if you don't it's hard to deal with life even if a thousand people "love you."

I always loved myself and had my head together. Then I realized after my brain injury I didn't have my head together anymore, which felt strange. I used to be a very STRONG PERSON.

So Tommy suggested that I should start seeing the therapist again. When I was in Magee Rehab I saw the therapist every day and when I left, I saw her once a week as an out-patient.

With a brain injury, people go through a personality change. They don't see the changes, just their family and friends see it. So it's normal with a brain injury not to be aware of any changes or problems.

So after a month of being home, I told my therapist I'm FINE—I don't need you anymore. She agreed in front of me because she knew what was happening. She and my husband (Rhona Cohen is her name) always talked because they knew I wasn't myself yet. That's why my husband always looked at me funny, I realized later.

I was so glad I was aware of what was happening to me.

They say nine out of ten couples and/or families break up after one has a brain injury. The person changes so much that the family and mainly the spouse feels like they are a completely different person.

I never understood this. When I was in the hospital, they kept telling me so many marriages break up after something like this happens. Now I can understand all that my husband, Tommy, went through with me. He thought, "SOMEONE CAME ALONG AND

TOOK CAROLANN AWAY FROM ME" people told me later that he used to say "the girl I was in love with isn't home anymore."

I wasn't the Carolann he used to know. I thank God everyday that I have a caring, loving, and patient husband. He was there for me ALL THE TIME and HE KNEW SOMEDAY, HE'D HAVE ME BACK AGAIN.

The best way he knew how was to WAIT and HOPE for me to realize what was happening. Thank God I did!

The brain is a funny thing. When someone breaks something you can see it. You know when it's doing better. Just by looking at it. You can't see the brain and no one knows what's going on inside there.

After I gained my weight back and looked like myself again—people constantly said you look <u>so good</u>—I cant believe you were ever in an accident. Especially because I pushed myself so hard. Everyone saw that I was doing so much! But mentally, I wasn't Carolann YET and only my family and my close friends knew that.

Another thing I was doing that I didn't know was hurting me at the time was that I was donating my time at Magee Rehab once or twice a week. I just went in each patient's room in the brain injury section. And I would just talk to them and say I was in your shoes at one time. That really helped them have confidence about themselves. Because they could believe seeing me the way I looked and how I was once lying in that bed only two months before.

It was really nice, talking to them. I just wanted to give a "bedside manner" to those patients. Because I knew I didn't get a bedside manner when I was there.

I used to walk home all the way smiling. I LOVED IT! ☺ Then I would go back to work the next day and HATE being there. Sometimes clients would complain about their hair.

One girl said once to me over the phone (calling the salon) "You took an inch off instead of half an inch. I'm devastated and I could kill myself." That made me crazy at that point hearing someone say that about half an inch of hair. I said, "I'm sorry, it will grow back in three weeks. It could have been worse." She answered very sarcastically, "how could it have been worse?" I said, "It could have been shaved off. You could have had an aneurysm."

That's when I knew I couldn't deal with it anymore. Normally, it's hard working with the public. Especially someone different in your chair every half an hour. But you are used to that and you laugh about it. Because you know if someone is not happy with their life or themselves they take it out on the hairdresser. So when I started talking to my therapist Rhona again, she said, "Carol, everything that is happening to you is normal. You basically have to learn everything again. Especially being socially appropriate. But don't worry, you're going to be alright. Just stoop pushing yourself and take it easy." Then she told me, "Carol, you're doing one thing wrong . . . donating your time at the hospital." I said, "Rhona, I love doing that." She said, "fine, but they are such different worlds. Between doing someone's hair and helping brain injured people, you are resenting someone talking about their hair." It's so trivial compared to someone whose brain is injured. So I stopped donating my time. I was shocked the first day I stopped. I went to my job the next day and I liked it again. I'm glad I spoke with Rhona, my therapist again because I would have never realized what I was doing wrong. Rhona's a really great person and smart too. Thank you, Rhona ☺.

It was so easy doing my job again. Even if I had someone that was in a bad mood in my chair, I was able to deal with that.

My boss Joan Pileggi is such a beautiful person. She is so helpful and caring to everyone. Thank God she understood all I went through. That made it so much easier for me. I could have had a boss who told me to leave. First of all, I was out four months. In this business, you lose clients even when you go on vacation for one week. So just taking me back after all that time—was so nice of her. She could have filled my chair with another hairstylist in a minute.

I lost a lot of clients in four months, 75% ☹ I was actually glad because I knew I wouldn't have been able to have been that busy with my energy level so low. So I booked myself every hour instead of every half hour.

After I thought I was doing better—which I wasn't—I booked every half hour again. After about a month, Joan spoke with me about what was happening. She knows me very well and noticed when I was doing a client, I looked like I couldn't wait till they got out of the chair. She was right, I couldn't. I was actually thinking about quitting. Everything was so hard for me then. So she suggested that I start booking every hour again. So I did, and it made a world of difference. Thanks Joan, you made an important part of my life EASY for me.

I was so happy I had my head together again. It was weird when I was going through all these changes. I actually felt like I was on drugs. I know about drugs. When I was growing up—which was the "hippie generation," a lot of people I knew were doing drugs everyday. I saw then how hard it I was for them to cope with life. How to have a normal conversation with people. Of course, I tried some drugs back then. That was the thing to do "being a hippie." It was fun at the beginning, just trying different things. You would just laugh and laugh. But I knew even then I didn't like what it was doing to me. It made me a different person. I liked me as my normal self. I liked being in control of myself. To know what I was doing. Also, seeing the people around me who really abused themselves really made me stop! ☺

Even now, I'm 34 years old and some of my friends still get high. Doing coke, smoking pot. It's a shame what they're doing to themselves.

A lot wonder why their lives are not together. They they're depressed a lot, etc. Messing with their brains is a bad thing to do.

A lot of people don't realize what they're doing to themselves. They think that after it wears off, they're fine. We don't know much about the brain. So how do we know what it's doing in there.

Having a brain injury messes up your brain, in many different ways. Some worse than others. Thank God mine wasn't that bad. Some people can't even remember their own mother, father, or husband. Some can't walk—talk. Or can't do the things they used to do.

Life is so short we don't even know if we're going to be here tomorrow. You just should take day by day—don't think about the past or the future. Just "BE HERE NOW."

So many people think of the past and how bad it was. Just say to yourself—that's life and what happened to me in the past was really bad—but it taught me a lot and made me a better person.

My girlfriend Michele Morroney's mom Marge used to say . . .

"IF IT DIDN'T KILL YOU, IT WILL MAKE YOU STRONGER."

Boy is she right about that. Taking day by day makes it so much easier because that's all we have to think about. That will make that day so much brighter and maybe even beautiful.☺

Another thing I found so important . . . don't expect other people to make you happy. Everyone wants a partner. They think by having someone that will make them happy. That's not true, you have to be happy with yourself first. Even if someone loves you to death, deep down you're not going to be hapy with yourself. So many people don't like themselves because they don't think they're pretty. You think that just being pretty is going to make you happy. Being pretty is not that important. Being a warm, loving, and caring person is what life is all about. So many people are selfish, they just think about themselves and NO ONE ELSE.

If you would think of other people and do for other people, that would make YOU HAPPY. Then good things will COME TO YOU. No one should EXPECT ANYTHING in life. People are constantly expecting things from other people or whatever and when it doesn't happen, they get so upset. The trick is, <u>DON'T EXPECT ANYTHING</u> and you will get surprises in life.

I cannot believe that I thought I was basically finished with my book. It has been one year and five months since my injury and I thought I got through the worst and was getting back to normal. As the days went on, I realized I did not like doing hair anymore. I was bored. People always open up to hair stylists, some even cry in your chair. I always liked that part of my job. The client not only chooses the hairstylist for his or her talent but also for his or her personality.

So when some clients would open up, I found myself wanting to say: "let's go sit somewhere else and talk." So as this was happening, it came to me one day. "I want to help people." So many people have emotional problems, I always enjoyed helping and sometimes wondered why they felt the way they did. I always thought it would be easy for them to change if they would just think differently. But only I knew what it felt like not to have my head together and to suffer emotionally and it was hard to get myself together alone. So I saw and see what it is like to see a psychologist weekly and how good you can feel. I think everyone should see a psychologist once in a while just to talk to someone—one who is on the outside looking in. you see things so differently. As all these feelings surrounded me for some time I decided to change my profession. I want to help people professionally, so I decided to go back to school and my goal is to get a PhD. in Psychology. I am now in college and enjoying it tremendously, which is so rare for me because I hated school with a passion

I was going to stay at Pileggi's while I went to school, but I knew that would be too hard to do. I wanted to put all my energies in school especially in the beginning, which paid off. I got B's and C's in my first semester, which again is rare for me because I used to get C's and D's I and some F's in school. What a change.

I believe that everything in life happens for a reason no matter how tragic. Not always for the best, but it happens for a reason. I think God was trying to tell me that I should be helping people.

When I left Pileggi's it was sad for me, I was there for eight years and I absolutely loved it. People could not believe a person could love their job so much. But of course, I wasn't liking it much anymore, so it really felt good to be sad when I left. I know if I did stay there while I was going to school, I would have left there, hating it and I didn't want that to happen. I wrote letters to my clients explaining that I was changing my profession, and wanted to give them notice that I was leaving. I also sent a card that I had made with my letter. Before I tell you what the card said, I want to explain how card came about.

When I was going through my awareness about being sarcastic to people, I heard this song that really moved me. My husband brought home a Van Morrison album with a song he heard and liked called "Someone Like You," which reminded him of me. So as we heard the album, another song came on that both of us had never heard. It was called, "I Forgot What Love was Like." This song really moved me, there was a phrase in it that really stuck to me. When the song was over, I said out loud "if my heart can do your thinking and my head begin to feel, I would look upon the world anew and know it is truly real." Tommy said, "What are you saying?" I told him that the song really moved me and I loved that phrase. He did not believe what was happening. One thing with brain injury is that your short-term memory is not too good. So for me to memorize what I had just heard was unbelievable. Well, I constantly said this to myself and would think about putting my heart in my head before I would speak to someone. What a difference this made because I spoke so mean to everyone—this actually made me think before I spoke, which I obviously stopped doing since my injury. So one day, I was walking down the street and I said to myself, what a beautiful world this would be if everyone would put their hearts in their heads before they spoke. People are always hurting people by things they say to each toehr. So

I got an idea I looked up and said thanks, Uncle Bill, you helped me again. My uncle Bill used to always carry this poem around in his pocket. When he found out he had cancer, he had cards printed of this poem and gave one to everyone he knew. It read:

On an ancient wall in China
Where a brooding Buddha blinks
Deeply graven is this message:
"it is later than you think!"
The clock of life is wound but once
And no man has the power
To tell just when the hands will stop
At late or early hour.
Now is the only time you own.
The past is a golden link
Go fishing NOW, my brother,
It is later than you think.

One side of this car was his name:

| Bill Ray | and the other side was the poem.

So I decided to also have a card printed to help people too. One side of my card was my name

| Carolann deBellis—DelColle | and the other side was

the verse from the song, which I changed "my" to "your"

> If your heart could do your thinking
> And your head begin to feel
> You would look upon the world anew
> And know what is truly real.

I also gave one to everyone I knew, hoping it would make them think before they spoke. This really did help me.

**THERE ARE NO ACCIDENTS
. . . IT HAPPENS AT THE
PERFECT TIME**

**MY INJURY WASN'T AN ACCIDENT,
IT WAS A MIRACLE**

**HOWEVER TOUGH LIFE GETS,
IT IS WORTH LIVING**

It has been ten years since I have looked at this book.
Boy have I changed. I am more tolerant, I used to fight with
people—just if they didn't agree with me.
I don't curse anymore—
I'm not as needy as I used to be.
I don't need a man by my side every minute to be happy.
I'm not as angry as I used to be.
I'm not as sexual as I used to be. Thank God!
And I'm not "so selfish" as I used to be—the other person comes first
most of the time ☺
I used to come first ALWAYS. My husband, Tommy used
to say . . . "If Carolann isn't happy, I'm not happy . . ."
"Neither is anybody else," he'd say.

I see things LOGICALLY AND CLEARLY NOW.

I'm a fun-loving caring person like I always was. People like being
with me again. I like being with me again.

They don't have that funny look on their faces as I'm talking to
them.

. . . nice things people say to me now . . . "Carol, it's so nice having
you here. You've been off Saturdays writing your book. You are quiet
when you work—but it's nice seeing you here." ☺

Mostly people I saw in work said that.

The nicest thing that happened is . . .

I DON'T TAKE OR NEED ANY MEDICINE NOW. I was on
anti-depressants "Zoloft"—lithium for cells I lost, so my blood level
needed to be high to grow more cells in my brain that I had lost.

It feels <u>so</u> good to be "sane" again. Not to be so so depressed and
want to just die like I always did. Thank you, Lord.

"Holding a cheerful attitude in mind and heart
is an important part of living a happy, joyful life."

"If your dreams die, you die."

I can now tell the rest of my story because I'm back to being my normal self ☺ logical—caring not the emotional person I was back then.

My mother says "you weren't crazy, you were just emotional." God bless her. She's my mother ☺. I was crazy and "out to lunch" in my eyes. I'm sure others' eyes too.

This is so easy now to write the rest of my story. I remember one of my clients, "Edith Shapin" . . . she's dead now unfortunately. She told me in 1987; when I told her I was writing a book . . . don't worry if it takes 20 years to finish this book, you may NEED to live your life first before you finish. So don't let it get you down if that happens. It's okay! Her statement to me is really helping me. Now—since it is now ten years after.

It was too emotional for me to write what I'm going to write now.

I keep a journal and many pieces of papers around so I wouldn't forget certain feelings. Even though I'd never forget what actually happened after my injury . . . while I was trying to live my life . . . that was PERFECT in my eyes and others' eyes.

BEFORE MY BRAIN INJURY, yes, my life was PERFECT . . . I had the perfect job in the most prestigious salon in Center City, Philadelphia. I worked right in the window. I was the first person people saw as they walked in. I loved the people I worked with—I loved my boss—I loved doing hair. Every half hour, a different person in my chair. I was never bored! Phenomenal money. Went to Paris and Italy every year. Paris to see the greatest hair show in creation.

I had the Best relationship, friendship and marriage anyone can ever have!
"Being married to your best friend"
what can be better . . .

ten years at that time of the accident, January 19, 1987. Great family, great friends. LOVED IT—LOVED IT—LOVED IT!!

Oh and don't let me forget . . . the best sex life. We were having sex 4-7 days a week. Sometimes 2-3 times a day. Even after ten years of being together. Unheard of!

. . . We thought . . . what's wrong with us? This is not normal. "let's not think about it," we'd say. We just love each other so much we can't keep our hands off each other.

We'd be at parties and just look at each other across the room and follow each other upstairs in a bathroom or closet and laundry room.

"How cheap . . ." we got caught once in cousin Michael's laundry room by him. While Michael was giving this fabulous party. So we weren't bored by any means. We just couldn't wait till we got home. Plus, diversion was nice ☺

then every time Tommy and I were missing, everyone would know what we were doing ☺ I guess we were obsessed with each other and sex. We also did it in the bathroom of an airplane as we were going to Italy . . . so small we thought, but we always found a way. ☺

I was always afraid of my man cheating on me. So I always tried to excite my husband at weird times. He'd come home and I'd be dressed in a sexy outfit . . . high heels, garter belt, etc. Wouldn't let him touch me before dinner . . . that drove him crazy. I'd do that at most once a month. So it wouldn't get to be a normal thing. Then two days before my accident, I sent Tommy a long red rose in a white box to his work. That read "meet me tonight at the Palace Hotel Room 102—Bring NOTHING BUT YOURSELF." No name was signed ☺ Tommy was still talking about that months after the accident. How exciting that was ☺ it was like having an affair but we were with each other! Of course he knew it was me even though I didn't sign my name ☺ We spent the night which was Saturday. Went home Sunday after breakfast. The accident happened Monday, the next day January 19, 1987-3 pm.

The next thing I remember next about me and Tommy's perfect relationship, friendship and marriage was . . .

He was sitting on one of our sofas and I was sitting on the other, facing him. He was just staring at me—not saying a word! It was a long stare. It wasn't a passionate stare—it wasn't a sexual stare. It was a weird stare. Like he didn't know me. Or something was going to happen.

Finally, after a few days of him doing that after work and after he cooked dinner . . . afraid to have me by the stove yet. I'd say, "why are you staring at me?" he'd shrug his shoulders or say I don't know. Is something going to happen to me—am I going to die—am I retarded—WHAT?! HE JUST STARED!!

March 26, 1987

Thursday first night home from Magee . . . we had sex after not having sex for two months . . .

It was beautiful having it again. But on having Tommy next to me—not sexual or passionate anymore ☹. My hormones had died after my brain injury. I was like a little girl inside. I didn't feel a thing . . . behavior got hurt in my brain—I wasn't aggressive anymore—I wasn't passionate anymore—I wasn't loving anymore—I wasn't sweet anymore . . . I was just there! I remembered sex but I felt nothing. They let us sleep together in Magee one night. We didn't have sex. We just snuggled—it was beautiful then home that night we loved it. But he and I didn't notice at that time that I wasn't sexual. Then one other time we did notice. I was loving him touching me so much—but I was just laying there enjoying him. But I was not moving—no sound—no nothing. Tommy just turned away and said, "you are not into this." I said, "I'm loving it." And I was. He just rolled over and went to sleep. What a difference from "the old Carolann and Tommy."

Then every night Tommy would come home. Come over to hug me and kiss me. I wouldn't not put my arms around him. He'd say, "why aren't you hugging me back?" I'd say, "I don't know." He'd just walked away.

He brought an X-rated movie home one night and wouldn't tell me what it was. Poor man was so horny. He needed sex badly. When I saw what it was, I ran in the bedroom. I felt like a little girl. "how can you take that in here," I said. We never needed X-rated movies in our lives. I was so upset. Not knowing what he was trying to do.

A male friend of mine said to me once . . . if your husband knew better, he would have grabbed your hand, walked you over to the sofa and treated you like a "virgin" again. Tommy didn't know how to do that with me. Because I wasn't a virgin when we dated. I was married before. I was extremely passionate. I was SO DIFFERENT NOW!

Tommy never forced me cause he said he'd feel like he was raping me. I was so passionate before. He couldn't handle me not being passionate anymore.

WE USED TO BE NUTS ABOUT ONE ANOTHER!!

Plus, Tommy was used to me taking charge. I actually controlled our relationship before. Not realizing that at the time. He was so used to me taking charge. Being aggressive, passionate. More like the man in the relationship. He felt like he was with a COMPLETELY DIFFERENT PERSON. God Bless Him!

I loved that Tommy wasn't a "macho bull-handed" man. I loved that he was so caring, so loving, so sensitive, so gentle.

So 19 months went by and Tommy and I still didn't have sex. I didn't miss it at all. My hormones were dead. Tommy came home every night. So I knew he wasn't cheating on me. I missed what we had. We weren't romantic anymore—WE DIED!

So I said to him one night, "what do we have? Something is missing? There's no romance." Even though I didn't miss sex physically, I missed us being passionate and romantic.

I FELT SO EMPTY.

So I suggested we'd separate and maybe we'd miss each other. Then maybe we'd get each other back—like we had each other before. Tears came down Tommy's eyes and I started to cry too. We both thought we'd wait till after Christmas. So our families wouldn't get so emotional.

Things got a little weird before he moved out. He started coming home late and wouldn't call. HEVER EVER DID THAT! I got so emotional about that. He'd say "I go to cousin Fred's after work to talk. I'm too upset to even call you—I don't know what I'm doing or what I want." So I learned to live with that and understand—sort of.

The first time he did that, my friend Debbie left her job at night cause I was crying so hard on the phone to her. I thought Tommy died or something terrible had happened to him.

January 1989, Tommy moved out. I found him an apartment in Center City where he wanted to stay. I was actually excited about this. We were getting along so well as friends. Deep down, not even deep down, I thought we'd miss each other so much—we'd be back together like we were before.

My psychologist Dr. Brenda Ivgar (I was still at Magee as an out-patient) who I liked very much, told me not to keep my hopes up. Tom may get out there and love it and NEVER COME BACK! I never thought that would happen—so I ignored Brenda's maybe prediction.

Life went on . . . I left Pileggis, I didn't like doing hair anymore. I wanted to help people inside their heads. Not the outside.

My doctor at Magee said, "your brain will never retain a thing." When I told him I was going to college to be a psychologist, well . . . I went back to school at 36 years old and was loving it. I really wanted to be there. I was paying for it—so that made me do well. I HATED SCHOOL IN THE PAST. I was getting B's and C's, which made me feel like I was smart. I was always intelligent "common sense wise."

But book—and school-wise, I always felt a little slow or maybe even dumb at times. I got "C's" "D's" and some "F's."

Thank God I'm strong-willed, determined, and aggressive. When the doctor said "your brain won't retain in school." I said, "WATCH ME." "I'll do it." And I did. ☺

I actually cried at times doing my homework. It was so hard to memorize. But I made it!

I thank God, I had a second chance to learn again. This felt SO GOOD to know after a brain injury I can go to school and get good grades.

. . . that's the only thing I didn't like about Magee—no confidence—they could at least say "I don't know, try, maybe it will work"—something?!

They are GREAT at rehabilitating you. I went from wheelchair to bars side by side to walker. Falling a lot, but they gave me the confidence to get right up!! ☺

I only would say 1-2 words at a time—I learned to read and retain again.

. . . it took two years before I was walking and talking well again.

Plus, I have a blind spot—left eye can't see side view. But I'm learning to deal with that also.

. . . I could have been blind or could have NEVER WALKED. These problems are not from my eye or my legs. This all comes from the brain.

I remember this girl sharing a room over with me at Magee. Here mother and two sisters were there everyday. She finally said . . . "Why are you people here everyday—what are you doing here?"

"I'm your mother, and these are your sisters." She had no idea who they were. She didn't believe them. So they brought pictures in. Childhood and all—she still didn't remember ANY OF HER PAST ☹ how sad. This made me feel so much better.

My long-term memory was with me. Short-term was bad. But at least I remembered my life! Thank you, Lord!

Speaking of "short-term memory" mine was so bad . . . Tommy would come in my room at Magee visiting me or reading to me. He'd do out in the hall to smoke or to the restroom. When he would return, I would say, "where have you been all day? I haven't seen you since last night." "Carolann, I was just here—I walked out for ten minutes"—I didn't believe him.

So I do understand why they have to ask questions that seem stupid. They need to see "how your brain is working." But they need to learn how to say it. So that we brain injured people don't feel like we're retarded. Again it's just like being raised again. You wouldn't want your child to feel stupid.

CONFIDENCE NEEDS TO BE PORTRAYED.

Ten years prior to my accident, people like me died. They didn't know how to save us. But things came a long way. They can now do wonderful things. But they still need to make us feel like we're not retarded or a child. Even though we are like children again. They need to give us confidence just like we are being raised as a child is.

I remember once a doctor said, "who's that next to you?" my mother answered. He asked me three times in one minute the same question. I was piss off, and answered, "how many times are you gonna ask me that f—ing question?" he made me feel so stupid. What he should have said was "Carolann, you may think this is stupid or wonder why I'm going to do this, but I need to ask you to see how your brain is functioning."

I remember being in group therapy at Magee. There was a guy who was paralyzed from a fall. he got real arrogant with me and said, "I fell off a roof, working three stories high. I could never walk again as long as I live. Your brain got hurt. Your brain will learn again and you will walk again—I won't."

I thought he was better off than me 'cause his brain didn't get hurt. And he only couldn't walk. God bless him. I realize today, I am better off 'cause my brain did learn again. I could do everything again. After really thinking about it. His brain did get hurt. He was so angry. I'm sure he will never be the same <u>ever again.</u> And he still can't walk. God bless him.

I remember being so angry in rehab. I was in Magee for two months. Knowing what was wrong with me. Knowing that I had to be there, but HATING IT! I was 34 years old and I felt like 64 years old. Everyone telling me what to do. I felt like it was <u>so much work.</u> Getting up—breakfast—shower—fix hair—make-up —go walking— therapy—hand therapy—writing therapy—art therapy. I felt like I was in school. I just wanted to lay in bed and stare at the TV.

. . . YOU'RE SITTING ON TOP OF THE WORLD—THEN ALL OF A SUDDEN, IT COMES CRASHING DOWN ☹

When people visited me, they would have a shocked look on their faces or they'd just fill up with tears. It was so depressing. I looked so different to them. First of all, I was 85 lbs, dropping from 110 lbs at 5'5" I was so skinny—I looked anorexic. My personality was so different. I couldn't hold a conversation. I didn't know what was happening to me. I didn't have my life anymore. I felt like an invalid. Plus I didn't remember my accident. So I couldn't even talk about it.

I HAD NOTHING TO TALK ABOUT. IT WAS SO DEPRESSING.

I remember being in work everyday doing hair and loving it.

I WANTED MY LIFE BACK.

So me being angry all the time. My nurses and therapists would say— If you want to get out of here, you need to work harder. So you can live your life again.

Well it took time for me to put my foot down and realize I was only hurting myself. So I started to love walking and doing everything to help me again. So I can go home and have my life back.

Then one day, I woke up and said "I'm ready to cut hair again." "You honestly think you can cut hair again?" nurses and Tommy asked. "I can do it with my eyes closed," I answered.

So Dr. Horn, God Bless him, came into my room the very next day and said "you think you can cut hair?" "yes," I said.

"Ok. I'll be your first customer."

Oh my God, I was so excited!! They set up a room for me. Tommy brought my tools in and I cut Dr. Larry Horn's hair. I WAS SO HAPPY. Of course—I knew what I was doing. I gave him a good haircut. They were so excited for me. They got me two-three people a day. I WAS IN ECSTASY.

So of course I thought I was ready for work. The aggressive, pushy person I was. "No way," they said, "you need to get your stamina back." Your balance needs to get better. You have to stand up to cut hair.

I didn't believe them. They said you can go home maybe by next week or so. Then come as an out-patient two-three times a week. And wait for at least six months until work.

I said you're crazy—I'm not waiting that long. So I went home after two weeks. Stayed home only one month and went back to work April 29, 1987.

I WAS SO EXCITED—I WALKED IN ON PILEGGI ON THE SQUARE, the best salon I have ever worked in fourteen years. All over my station there were balloons and a welcome back sign on my mirror. So sweet, I was touched! My station was right in front of the salon at the window. Everyone that walked in saw me first. The people who knew me gasped as they walked in. shocked to see me after three months and twelve days. Then shocked to see how skinny I got. I was about 95-100 lbs. I gained 15 lbs in two months before because I was eating normally again. So I though it looked fine, going from 80-95-100 lbs. But I obviously didn't look fine to everyone else. Being macrobiotic before the accident eating no red meat, dairy, or sugar. Not because I wanted to get thinner (was always 120-125), I just wanted to be healthy. Being a hairdresser, I got 3-5 colds a year plus strep throat or the flu a year. Plus I wanted to live forever ☺.

Everyone used to say . . . everyone you know will be dead—you'll be the only one alive ALONE ☺

. . . and I almost died in the accident!

. . . What a Beautiful Welcome ☺

1st day back at work ☺

After my accident, I realized I could die anytime, "when it's meant to be." No matter what I ate. So I stopped being a "health fanatic." I started eating anything I wanted. I exercise four days a week and I feel great.

I am now 126 lbs at 5'5". Still thin, but not too thin. I can't believe I let myself look like that. "no body fat at all." My breasts went from 31 AA to 34 B ☺

I like how I look now—I'm really healthy.

Before my accident, I worked five days every half hour with a new client in my chair. I used to do 12-16 clients in 7-8 hours and one day a week 9-10 hours 16-22 clients a day. Joan thought I shouldn't push so I worked three days and did one client an hour instead of two. I agreed. I was just SO HAPPY TO BE BACK!!

I lost 75% of my clientele. Even when you take off a week for vacation you lose clients. So if your client is happy with whoever cut their hair they go back to that stylist. It's something hairdressers understand. We lose—we gain. After time went on, my feelings got hurt. Most of my clients were in the chair next to me. They felt funny seeing me—so they'd just ignore me. I really felt like I came down the Totem Pole. And boy was I high on it before the accident!

I lost my personality when I was cutting hair—I couldn't cut and talk at the same time. Clients would always ask, "are you okay? You're so quiet." So I lost more people. They come to you for your talent; your personality. Well my ego couldn't handle it anymore. It wasn't the money I was glad to be alive. Even though I lost 75 or more percent of the money I used to make.

At this point, everyone in my family wanted me to sue the company van that hit us. I really didn't want to—I was just glad to be ALIVE. Plus I thought I'd eventually make good money again.

So they finally talked me into it.

My life did change—lost good money at job—lost husband, lost friends, lost energy—lost memory, had to always write notes to remember—lost hormones—they said hormones may never come back.

I used out of court, made 320,000. My lawyer said if I sued in court, I could have made maybe a million. But I'm alive—what's money?

Thank God I now have money coming in the rest of my life—invested in stocks and bonds and have a financial advisor. Because I know I wouldn't be able to work like I sued to. My tolerance level is still not good!

I gave Tommy 50,000 of my money. I felt like he deserved that because he lost his wife and the friend he knew and loved ☹ So after Tommy and I were separated, maybe a month or two, I went to his apartment. I visited for a while. We talked nicely then we made love. It was nice being next to Tommy again, but we still didn't love like before ☹.

Time went on; we didn't talk much. He was living his life obviously content because he hardly called. I was missing my life with him so much. I wanted to die! Love and a relationship was so important to me. I needed a man to love me. I was married most of my life. I was 21 when I married my first husband of five years. I started dating Tommy only three months after my break-up. So I was used to, and loved, a man in my life. Then guess what happened . . . my hormones came back. I found myself walking down the street one day and I was looking at every man's crotch. I said to myself "what the hell is happening to me?" down below was actually throbbing constantly. I was going crazy.

If I wasn't raised the way I was, I know I would have been a very loose woman. Thanks, Mom and Dad.

I called Tom and told him. He couldn't believe it. The doctors said 'her hormones may never come back.' Alleluia!! I was so happy.

I felt like a human again. So I said to Tom, could you come here and have sex with me at least once a week? He said, "I have to think about it Carolann."

I called him the next day "so what do you think?" he told me he didn't think it was a good idea. Because I'd be depressed when he would leave. I agreed but I was so disappointed. Boy was I horny. I actually took care of myself seven to ten times a day. The feeling wouldn't go away I always satisfied myself, but it was like the first time I ever had that feeling. I needed a man so badly. Plus I think since I had feelings again, I was so used to sex with Tom every day before. So I always wanted it.

I knew this was insane masturbating seven-ten times a day and I always wanted it. I was constantly talking about sex and masturbating. When I think about it now, I could die. Such a personal ting to talk about.

Finally, Aunt Ida helped me. Why don't you go to a sex store and buy a boy? You obviously miss a penis. So I did. I went and looked in the case for one that looked the size of Tommy ☺. I bought it and boy what a difference! I was so satisfied I only had to do it once a day. Then once a week. Much much better! Thanks, Aunt Ida.

Then I was dying again. I wanted Tommy back. He was dating his ass off. My psychologist Brenda was right. I started calling him everyday. He blocked my calls. I went to pay phones so I could get through. I was calling him three-five times a day. I drove that poor man crazy. Then one day, I was walking to his apartment to see him and talk. So on the way, I saw our car parked across the street from the health food store we shopped in. there was a blonde sitting in my seat. I died when I saw this. I asked Tom never to come around where I go or where I live with a girl. Because I know I would die if I ever saw that. He told me he wouldn't. so I crossed the street. Checked her out. Walked to the back of the car, waiting for Tom to come out of the store. I was going to get in the backseat. But the doors were locked. I just wanted to break it for him and make his life crazy. Because he didn't want me anymore.

Tom walked out of the store—saw me—and said, "what are you doing?" "You have a lot of nerve putting someone in my seat." "We're separated, Carolann." "Get her out," I said. He tried to talk low so she couldn't hear. The windows were closed. He pulled my arm and dragged me down the street. A cab came by and he tried to push me in it after stopping it, "saying I don't love you anymore Carolann." I pulled away, he grabbed my arm again—so I wouldn't run to the car . . . knowing that's what I was trying to do, to throw her out of my seat.

All of a sudden, not knowing I was going to do this, as he was holding my arm . . . my mouth just went down to his arm and I bit it. He couldn't get my teeth away. I was biting so hard. After about a minute, blood was dripping down his arm and he pulled away. He then ran away to the car, jumped in and started it. I ran after him like a maniac! Before he pulled away, I jumped on the hood in front of his window. That's when the girl saw me. I was screaming "get her out of my seat." "get off" he screamed and kept screaming until he finally pulled away and I fell off.

Then I walked to his apartment 16-18 blocks away. I sat on his steps for two hours. He never came home. A week later, I went again and sat from 5 am to 8 am waiting until he left for work. I KNEW I HAD LOST IT THEN. When he saw me—he told me he didn't want to come back—he didn't love me and he didn't want a divorce! I guess he would feel really bad if he divorced me. He ran to his car and pulled away. I was going crazy! I WANTED TO DIE OR I WANTED HIM DEAD!

. . . every single day, I thought of him and how I would kill myself. Or how I would kill him. I knew I could never kill him. But I made so much money—I could get someone to do it. I was scaring myself. So I went to talk to Brenda after thinking about this for a week—every minute. I brought Aunt Ida with me. Brenda told me as soon as I told her. I think you should go to the psychiatric ward at Hahneman Hospital. I said yes, I want to do that. Aunt Ida said, "Brenda, do you really think Carolann needs to go there?" "Yes," Brenda said, "Ida, she wants to kill herself."

. . . one thing that stopped me from killing myself then was . . . if I slit my wrist, there'd be so much blood. I wouldn't want my family to have to have that devastation of finding me. Then I thought about taking all my pills. Taking the whole bottle may kill me. I heard if you do that you throw up unbelievably. I didn't want that mess to be there either. Thank God I thought that way. Besides, the main reason I didn't was . . . I COULD NEVER DO THAT TO MY FAMILY! When somebody dies in our family, we die!

If I kill myself, my whole family would never be the same. And I know they'd never forgive me. That made me tell Brenda that I definitely needed help.

After sitting on Tom's step for 3-4 hours, I called my sister Renee to tell her what I had done. She already knew that I bit his arm the week before.

She told me if I didn't get help and stop this nonsense, I would never be allowed to see her son Franke anymore. Because I wasn't right. She just wouldn't want me around him. My nephew who I loved so much was one and a half years old. That woke me right up.

I entered Hahneman University psychiatric ward a couple of days later. THAT WAS THE BEST THING I COULD HAVE EVER DONE!! Brenda was right as usual.

There were real crazy people in there. Just looking around at them, you could see they weren't right. Aunt Ida came that day. She wanted to die. She said to me, "do you want to be here?" I said, "yes, I have to, Aunt Ida."

I stayed seven days—had my own room—told them I must have my own room. We had group therapy three times everyday. And one on one with a doctor everyday.

I thank God I did this.

I found Carolann was nothing without a man. And I would die if I didn't have one. Not any man—I am picky, Thank God. I wanted Tom back ☹.

I always though I was "my own person" independent, loved and liked myself, loved life to the max . . . but I found out I never knew (obviously hiding from myself) Carolann wasn't ANY OF THESE THINGS WITHOUT A MAN LOVING HER. WOW, WHAT A BREAKTHROUGH.

Thank you, Lord for making me see the light. ☺

I thought I lost myself when I lost my marriage. But I found after . . . I never actually found myself until I lost my marriage ☺.

My LOVING FAMILY who I LOVE DEEPLY . . .
Me, my sisters . . . Janice and Renee
At Aunt Louise's ☺ 1989

Janice—Renee—Me
1988
Renee's Surprise 30th Birthday ☺

Mommy & I at Campo's house
W/ Mike . . . his Store Campo's on wall
"Campo's Deli"

Daddy & I on my Wedding Day
1981

Me & Aunt Jean

Me, Cousin Maureen

Uncle Buster (Mom's Brother)
Aunt Jilda

Uncle Dante, Mom
Aunt Augusta (Dante's Mom)—Who
I saw when in Coma, Died 75
Uncle Ralph 1960's

Billy, Me, Michelle, Michael, and
Aunt Jean In Avon Connecticut 1960's

Me & Mommy
1980's

My Birthday 1990
Denise, brother-in-law Frank, Michele,
nephew Franke, Mia, Me, Michael-Ann-Lindsay,
Dad and Janice through mirror 1990

Family gathering at my place . . .
Frankie, Janice, Uncle Dante, Dan, Renee,
Michael, Aunt Jean (holding Deanna)
Mom, Uncle Frank, Aunt Louise (holding Aleida), Fred,
Angela (holding Michael-Ann), Bobby (holding Maureen) ☺
1993

Mommy with Jan, Rudy, Renee, Me, jan's twins Aleida and
Deanna, Jan's husband Dino in the back . . . who we lost. ☹
1995

My Dear Friend "Celeste"
Friends since 9th grade 1968

My Dear Friend "Denise" & I at my Wedding ☺
(Friends since 1st Grade 1960 ☺)

"Michele" Friends since 9th grade
1968

Michele & her Mom "Marge" who I loved DEEPLY
. . . at their Wildwood crest house ☺

I'd like to share with you a log I kept from Hahneman psychiatric ward and questionnaire that helped me.

My stay in Hahneman University Psychiatric ward: 7 days

A log I kept in group therapy three times a day.

"practice"

the responsibility of the relationship

who I am
who they are
and what they make me in the relationship

just
love her serve her affirm like her appreciate adore acknowledge her

being related . . .
who do you need to be to get an invitation to passion

have to practice it. The principals. Distinguishes to give the possibilities of playing.

If I am I because you are you
And if you are you because I am I
Then I am not I
And you are not you
~ Old Hassidic saying

I—we

Avoiding the domination of the other person
Relationships . . . getting it back to where it used to be . . . it never works that way.

The issue of me being related . . . is that I need to be patient when I am being criticized and also to open to listening—without getting extremely defensive.

I would like to give more than I expect to get back.

Issues: youre ignoring how you feel and youre just thinking of him . . . doing too much or loving intently or taking advantage of someone leaving you so intently.
~ Another looking at me and him on screen.

A fool
A taker
~ Me looking at me on screen

when I'm not able to play in a relationship

when someone says something to me I don't like hearing or don't agree with, defensism or I get sad.

"love" and "sex" has nothing to do with each other. Nothing

love does not have a limit

love doesn't need to be afraid

love is just to be allowing

ex. A chicken had pepper rubbed on her belly and went looking for a rooster it was real nice . . . next day the chicken didn't get pepper rubbed and the rooster passed and the chicken kicked him—rooster said . . . what did I say

cannot love someone when you are making them wrong!

What makes you the judge (did you get a phone call from God?) to say you're right.

We thought we were in love . . . but we were only in lust There's nothing wrong you're not the judge.

You're not accepting no need you can accept anything . . . allow that to be.

Our issues never change.

Where are your relationships located

Nature of a conversation that is giving you the relationship between you too. Also you are giving about yourself to the other person. And vice versa.

"internal conversation" what I'm having to myself about them

. . . now I love this person so much and how I cant want them to feel this. How I will do anything for them because they are as important to me as I am to myself.

Get off it!

IT DOESN'T MEAN ANYTHING
SO GET IT!

Work relationship
I am willing to have in this relationship . . .
Friendliness
Compassionate
Happiness
Good feedback
Good feelings
Contentment

What is possible . . . good feedback.

Who could I possibly be in this relationship?

If I feel better about myself, all of their talk wont bother me. I can actually ignore!

  I could be a kind, considerate, fun-loving person.

The other person or persons are happy—contented and nice people that I like to be around.

A certain culture—brought two or three cows a wife: Johnny bought eight cows for his wife. people couldn't believe how plain she was. A certain person went to this island to see her.

  He could believe not believe how gorgeous she was

He told him about the rumors around and asked?! Johnny said it was true but I would never buy three cows for my wife so I bought eight which no one has ever done.

Therefore she became and grew into a beautiful, beautiful woman!

Invitation to passion

No attraction

No love

No compassion

Do not let passion be involved with these . . .

Its very different from passion

How much of myself I'm willing to be here—willing to engage.

Praying for passion is like a hen praying for pepper. Not important!

If wanting passion, invitation to I'd walk in the room—very seductively what would I'd say—boy are you sexy! I'd love to be passionate with you.

Does not need to be sexual

Romance

. . . is a mental and physical bond between two people Webster says it's a made-up story (a fictitious tale of wonderful and extraordinary events). Story made p.

I meet this beautiful sexy prince of a man by the river. He was standing there alone as I was walking by. Our eyes met and we just stared at each other very intently. Then I could not walk by him. I stopped, he grabbed my hand and we walked just staring at each other. We stopped and started kissing. It felt like it was for hours. I think it was.

What I got out of today's seminar is . . . I am 100% responsible for my happiness and my relationship.

. . . I don't have a relationship now and I'm very sad about that. But I know someday when I am supposed to I will . . . and we will look into each other's eyes and know that we are supposed to be together.

Questionnaire:

I need: ~~health~~ . . . to help people professionally

My future is: ~~uncertain~~ . . . exciting

My big trouble is: ~~health/pain~~ . . . my mother and father's future

What I want most of all is: ~~no pain, good health and love~~ . . .
everyone to be happy

I failed: ~~never~~ . . . never

If I am forced, then I will: ~~fight for understanding~~ . . . work
somewhere I don't like to

People are: ~~human~~ . . . human

I fear: ~~vulnerability~~ . . . nothing

My life so far has been: ~~Chalienging~~ . . . hard, happy, and learning
so much

When I have a problem, i: ~~think~~ . . . think and talk about it

I often feel badly about: ~~lack of mobility~~ . . . people's unhappiness
especially everyone I love

I often feel like: ~~crying~~ . . . doing

I think that I am: ~~intelligent~~ . . . a warm, caring, and happy person

I get upset when: ~~I am overwhelmed~~ . . . when my husband's
not happy

What I dislike very much is: pain . . . people not being happy
about life in general

When I want something very much, I will: ~~ask for it~~ . . . try very
hard until it happens

My heart often feels: ~~open~~ . . . very happy and warm

Fathers are: ~~parents~~ . . . wanting their children to be happy

Mothers are: ~~parents~~ . . . love, giving, and wanting much for
their children

My childhood was: ~~intense, but made me strong~~ . . . intense, but
made me strong

What disturbs me is: ~~pain~~ . . . someone caring about material
things, rather than feelings

My problems are: serious . . . none
The one thing that I would never do is: ~~treat anyone with disrespect~~ . . . make someone unhappy intentionally
When things become difficult, I: ~~pray and read~~ . . . relax, read or pray.
When I disagree with another person, I: ~~listen~~ . . . usually tell them

If my heart could do my thinking and my head begin to feel, I

would look upon the world anew and know what is truly real.

Van Morrison

I came home. I still saw Brenda once a week and finally started taking anti-depressants like they always wanted me to after I came home.

My life was saved again!

So I went through thinking about Tom every minute like I used to do. Still hoping someday we may return together. but going on with my life. I was jealous he was dating—it was so easy for him. He worked at a bar and restaurant and met girls all the time. Unfortunately for him that girl in the car stopped seeing him after my explosion. Sorry, Tom.

I met no one. Everyone my age was married. so guess what

I did . . . I called a dating service. I had five dates in three months. Each man was nothing to look at. No personalities and obviously desperate men who cannot find anyone. So they have to pay to find me. They were all shy. They hardly talked. All took me to dinner first then everyone asked as they drove me home. Can I come in—"for what," I asked. "To get to know you better." Yeah right, they obviously wanted sex cause they paid for the date. Give me a break! I paid $300 for that and learned another lesson . . . I'd rather be alone on my sofa depressed than go out with just anybody. I was still not feeling great but my medicine helped me deal. I didn't want to kill myself anymore. And I didn't want Tom dead anymore. So life was a little better.

Plus I was able to find out more about me. Which I needed to do. I got really close to God. He was in my heart ALWAYS! I would cry sometimes and say aloud . . . "God, I know I'm learning from this. This is supposed to happen. I trust you." That kept me alive!

My biggest fear was not having a man to love me. Growing up was rough at my house. There was a lot of love. But my mom and dad weren't always happy with each other. My dad cheated on my mom a few times. She was so unhappy at those times . . . that was my biggest fear. To be unhappy because of a man.

So I think I always looked for a man who I thought would NEVER CHEAT ON ME.

I got married the first time thinking I was "in love." Joe DiJohn loved me so much. I knew he would never cheat on me. So I felt safe—I LOVED HIS FAMILY—and I was ready to get out of my house at 21 years old.

As time went on, I found I wasn't in love with him. I was just n love with love. So I broke it off after five years. I didn't even know myself yet!

"If I'm making a mistake, I need to make it."

"When it gets the darkest, that's when the stars come out." Three months passed as I was trying to get to know myself. Then my door bell rang 11:00 one night. It was Tommy; ☺ he was a friend I knew since 7th grade. I was shocked! He said I was just at the "homestead" (a bar in our neighborhood we all hung at" "I heard you and Joe were separated," he said. "yes," I said. He then said, "I always liked you—I always wanted to go out with you. But I was either involved or you were," he said. "when I heard you were getting married, I was going to do the "graduate" come to church and stop it." He said. Then he said, "I knew you weren't in love with Joe—you just wanted to get out of your house." I said, "but you are going out with Karen." "I don't love her and she wants to get married. I like you." Then we sat on my sofa and he tried to kiss me. I didn't let him do that. I wasn't ready to get involved with any other man. Plus he was seeing someone.

He left and called me three months later to say he had broken up with Karen and wanted to see me. THE BEST RELATIONSHIP OF MY LIFE STARTED OUT AT THIS POINT. I just knew it. ☺ of course, I didn't let Tommy touch me for three-four months. I was 24-25 years old. I was mesmerized by him. He was always my friend. So we were extra close because we knew each other so well. He is my friend Denise Campo's cousin plus his grandmother and mine were friends.

We loved to dance. The disco era had just started. Boy did we have fun!!

Tommy was mesmerized too; he wanted to get married after six months to a year. I wasn't even divorced yet. No way did I want to marry yet. And I was still trying to know who I was. I waited four years before marrying Tom. Although we were together almost every night.

As life went on with Tommy and I, I had no complaints. It was ABSOLUTELY PERFECT.

He did everything for me—he always said yes. He was so romantic. I would sometimes find a card in the mail refrigerator after he left for work. For no reason, just a car. Life was great with my friend & husband. But after all that was said and done . . . I realized that I controlled Tommy.

One time we had a fight, he said, "you love yourself more than you love me." I said, "If I didn't love myself first how in the hell could I be able to love you?" he answered, "I love you more than I love myself." I knew he was in trouble then. And an insecure man I found him to be ☹.

Tommy then told me he'd be the best husband and friend I can ever have.

Tommy was my puppet. Great at the time. I didn't realize he was my puppet.

I still didn't see or find myself yet. I needed Tommy to love me and adore me. To make me happy and content with myself and with my life. I loved him so much.

Tommy's song to me was

"When a man loves a woman"

by Persey Sledge

. . . he'd lip sync this part of it all the

time to me . . . "when a man loves a woman

he can never do her wrong,

he'd never want another girl.

When a man loves a woman

He'd get down on his knees and pray,

Say goodbye to his best friend

If he'd put her down . . .

There was so much love between us. It was the most beautiful feeling I ever had in my life. I would watch him looking at me at times with so much love in his eyes. Whew, what a feeling.

I'll never forget our wedding songs . . . "you are my friend" by Patti LaBelle that we slow danced to. And "never knew love like this before" by Stephanie Mills that we fast danced to. I still get chills when I hear them ☺.

The last thing I remember before going on with my life was a telephone conversation with

Tom   .   .   .

"I'm not in love with you anymore Carolann," he said as he was crying.

"I just want to love someone so bad," I said. "it's easy for you. You're a man. You like clubs, you like bars, you like girls. So you can always shave fun. You are a perfect atmosphere. You don't want to live with anyone 'cause you're always meeting new girls."

Tom, "I'll leave you alone—you can call me when you want your records and tapes. I then told him I didn't understand why all of you . . . Debbie, Bianca, and you just let me go. I know I've changed. But all I am is too emotional. I say everything I feel. I used to be strong as a bull. I can't believe you all just forgot about me! I need new friends that know me now and not before.

"Bye Tom," I said.

"Bye Carol," he said, real sad.

. . . a week later, I got this note . . .

Carolann, I'm truly sorry I can't "be there" for you—I hope all is well.

Then I wrote him this letter.

Tom,

It's been so long—think its about time . . .

I'm sorry for making you feel bad on the phone. When I get hurt, I get so sad and I guess that's how I want you to feel. I honestly still think you're my friend and need you to help me in my emotional outbursts. But unfortunately you can't. plus you're still so full of guilt! Get over it! I finally understand it's impossible for us to be friends. Such is life. And honestly, Tom, I don't want you back. It's too different now and we changed so much, I don't even think the sex would be good anymore . . . too much has happened all the way around.

So 'm sorry I called you bald. That wasn't nice. And I hope to god for you that you are stronger.

God bless you, Tom.

Love Carolann

. . . I Thank God I have the MEMORIES . . .
Tommy & I . . . when "Baby Bangs" were in ☺
1982

Tommy & I celebrating w/ friends in a limousine
Florida 1983

Tommy & I in Paris, France
1984

Tommy & I at his sister Lorraine's
house on Christmas 1985

At this time, a song was out that really hit me. When I knew it was over. I don't have the heart to hurt you it's the last thing I want to do. I don't have the heart to love you the way you want me to. Then another song, "it must have been love but it's over now" by Whitney Houston. That really did it. I knew it was over.

Finally I let him go.

If you love someone, let them go. If he doesn't return, he wasn't yours. If he does, he's yours. So obviously, he was never mine and I'm glad I found out.

Life went on. It was hard. I was depressed. I had to do something. So I decided to go to bartending school. I wanted to work and have fun again. I left college realizing school would take too long to finish. Before I became a psychologist. And it was hard to memorize for tests. Dr. Lawrence Horn was right! Thanks, Dr. it took a year for me find that out.

I went and met my bartending teacher.

Andrew, he was Italian. He was good looking and he was nice. "I liked him instantly." I'm Italian and always liked going with Italian men. We understood each other—we were the same. When I paid for that stupid dating service, I said that they must be Italian or at least half Italian. Not a one was Italian ☹ . . . they just had dark hair and "could be."

So I was excited to meet an Italian man I liked.

As the week went on, I realized I was attracted to this man.

The very first man I was attracted to since Tommy—one year prior.

Andrew and I got close. We became good friends. Three months passed and school was done. But I still went and visited him at school. Anyone can sit in after they graduated so I went at least once a week. It was nice and fun to be close to a man again that I liked.

Andrew knew I was still in love with Tom so we remained just friends. All I did was talk about sex. So he teased about sex a lot. We were very comfortable around each other. I loved that he called me "Carolann." Many people just call me "Carol" except my family.

I was getting to know Andrew better and liking him very much.

Even though I was talking bout sex so much, I didn't just want sex. I WANTED LOVE AGAIN!

Andrew was in a sort of relationship with a girl in school. We all got real close. She liked him more than he and wanted more. So they stopped seeing each other. Then a few months after he married a close friend of his. Boy was I shocked!

WHO KNOWS IN LIFE!

One day, Andrew's blender broke in school. He called me to borrow mine until he bought one. Then it happened . . . we started kissing in my kitchen. Then went to the bedroom and had sex. After me not having sex in two years—this was very very nice. ☺ and fulfilling. We went on for two years. I saw him at least once a week. Sometimes three times a week. We never went out. He just came to my condominium, after his day job. An hour or two before he taught bartending. Or I'd meet him at school before he started. You know what happened ☺.

I know I was doing wrong by being with a married man. I didn't know his wife. so I thought that was fine. I didn't feel guilty. I also felt God understood because Andrew kept me alive.

I needed attention from a man I liked him so much. I had so much fun with him and felt so fulfilled.

I think deep down I thought he'd leave his wife for me. How could he be happy with her if he was with me 1-2-3 times a week.

After being married only 4-5 months. Time went on with Andrew. It finally bothered me that he wasn't my man. Even if he left his wife and lived with me, I would always think he'd be cheating on me. I believe "once a cheat, always a cheat."

I wanted love again so badly. I was starting to get real depressed again. I was so lonely I could have died. I realized sex was absolutely NOTHING without being in love. I needed and wanted sex badly because I was used to it with tom 4-7 days a week. Even though it was four years since Tom and I had had that perfect relationship. I was used to sex so much when I had a man in my life. Plus I was always very sexual.

It was great for the moment when I was with Andrew. It was definitely <u>more than sex</u>. It was actually beautiful but I know I couldn't have him ever. Andrew was not a monogamous person. I need and want a monogamous person in a relationship.

I still went on with Andrew until my mother opened my eyes. I was in the process of adopting a child. Already gave $100 for them to start the procedures. My mother knew about Andrew—not happy mind you. Especially having my dad cheat on her in the past. My mom said to me, one phone call . . . "you shouldn't be adopting a child. You're just lonely and want a man. It's going to be so hard. You're 38 years old, you're going to be a single parent. You will never find a man raising a child." Then she said (it was like the Blessed Mother came down to tell me) . . . "what you're doing with Andrew is absolutely wrong!!" "but I would rather see you go on with him than you adopting a child. Boy did that statement affect me! I hung up and called the adoption agency, canceled the procedures. I lost the $100, didn't care! Then I sat down and wrote a letter to Andrew. Then just out of the blue, I wrote a poem from the letter I wrote. I never wrote a poem in my life, so this was weird to me and very exciting.

I went to see Andrew in person and said to him . . .

"Andrew, I can't see you anymore. This must end." "Ok," he answered. I said, "I wrote a poem for you. But before I read it, to you, I first want to say, I do not look down on you. I don't think you're scum. I actually feel bad for you. I'm the one who made this last two and a half years."

"I'm feeling bad today, but I must say goodbye." If things were different and you weren't married, and if you wanted me—only me for the rest of your life. I'd be with you in one second." "I know you care about me. I know you love me—not <u>in love</u> but you love me. You are very special to me, Andrew. You will always be here (pointing to my heart), always, baby."

Then I read my poem . . .

Just Like Dad

I walked in the room
He was sitting there
But no big deal . . . I didn't stare
He seemed nice but my heart didn't flare.
Because I knew my "x" was still there.
He started teaching class and to my surprise
My first love of my life was in my eyes.
Since all my hurt and all my pain
This is the first time I felt myself gain
I loved how he talked. I loved how he was
We became very close, yes, that's how it was.
As life went on
He took a wife
I was so shocked
But I didn't thrive
One day he called his blender broke
We went into my kitchen and he started his mission we kissed
for so long, I loved every minute
But then he had to go 'cause something was in it
Something I really didn't want to happen that day
And for two a half years, I couldn't get away.
I fell in love and wanted him for life
But finally realized he wasn't my type

I wasn't hurt, I wasn't sad.
I just came to know
He was just like my dad
I could never trust, like my mom couldn't too
And I'd always wonder
Where he'd be buckling his shoe

He just looked at me after I had read it to him. "I want you to have it," I said. I handed it to him, we hugged, and I left. I felt so good 'cause I knew I had to get along and go on with my life . . . and I thanked God for Andrew.

My love for Tom still was strong when I felt emptiness. My feelings go back to us and I miss that very very much.

I was actually "in love" three times in my life. Once when I was 16 with Chalie Sage—a neighborhood guy. I was 15-16-17 years old with Tom at 26 years old, and with Andrew at 37 years old.

And I know I could be happy the rest of my life with one of these men. If the circumstances were different.

I again thank God for this because some people were never in love one time. Loved someone yes, but "in love," no. there is a difference!

I never though it would love or be in love with anyone after my first love at 16 . . . but I was. After Tommy, I never never ever thought I could ever love or be in love like that again. Until Andrew came along as a friend and as a lover. And he was better at both surprisingly so . . . Lord above!

Now I think if I found someone after Tom how in the hell am I going to find the same feeling with another man. I guess what will be will be. And there is nothing on this earth I can do about it.

Guess what . . . I found someone! I knew Jerry Durante almost twenty years. Another guy from my neighborhood. Remember my hormones were back, I wanted sex always . . . I was at a party and Jerry was there. I was never really attracted to Jerry but always liked him. He was funny and everyone love him. All of a sudden, I was looking at him talking to everyone walking, sitting, laughing, and I said out loud next to my friend Rita Francis. "oh my God. Jerry is so sexy. I never noticed. Rita answered, "yes he is, you two would be great together." "yes, wouldn't that be nice." I said. I didn't say another word about Jerry that night. A week later, I was at the same house Chalie and Mary's. Jerry walked in to go to a bar in the neighborhood to get a sandwich, Chalie decided not to come. So me, Jerry, and Mary went to the Homestead. Mary went to the ladies room and I looked at Jerry and said, "I need to tell you something, Jerry Durante. I was never attracted to you, but I loved you as a person. You were always Jerry. You made me laugh and I loved being around you. I loved Tom so much I guess that's why I never noticed." "noticed what?" "you are so sexy. I cant believe I never noticed." His eyes and mouth opened really wide. "You are!" I said. The night progressed. Nothing happened. We saw each other maybe two-three times after that he acted like Jerry, didn't make a move. Of course, I was waiting. Then I wanted him so badly, I went and bought Tony Bennett tickets. They were $49.00 a piece. Now I know what guys do when they want sex. I called and told him we were going to see Tony Bennett. I told him he can sleep over 'cause he lived in Wildwood an hour and a half away. His mother lives twenty minutes away but he can still stay. He said fine. I was so excited, I knew I was going to have sex with Jerry and I was so excited. We went; it was great, we went for a few drinks after. I WAS READY. We were back at my condominium. He sat on one sofa, I sat on the other. I started talking about sex as usual. I brought up something about Andrew and a pair of panties I wore or had. He asked are you wearing those panties now? I answered I'm wearing better ones now. And I stood up and lifted my skirt to show him. I felt so comfortable with him, it didn't phase me a bit what I was doing. Plus a few drinks! I showed him the front, then I turned and showed him the back. They were "g-string panties" so he saw my backside. I turned around and fixed my shirt. Then I sat down like nothing happened. Within three minutes, he came over to my sofa, sat down next to me and said as he pointed to his crotch, ""he wants you real bad." I looked at him with such excitement. The he pointed to his head and said, "but he can't." "why?" I said. 'Cause of Tom. "Tom," he said, "is with your cousin! Your CarolAnn DeBellis and you don't F . . . CarolAnn DeBellis unless she's your girlfriend or your wife." I died and went to heaven when he said that. What respect he had for me. I actually fell in love with Jerry that night. Jerry slept in my bed that night. I slept with just my g-string panties on and nothing else. He slept with a pair of sweatpants and a t-shirt. "could it be" he was like the girl—I was like the guy. In the middle of the night, Jerry awoke and started making out with me, as he got on top. I said "yeah" to myself. Then all of a sudden, he got off of me, turned away and said, "I can't."

The next morning, I said, "what happened last night?" he answered, "I woke up and said where am I—that's Carol. Let me pretend her name is Judy. And i started but I just couldn't. it was you." I love that man—respect is so important to me. Plus I was brain injured still a bit so I guess he didn't want to take advantage. Plus he told me later—I never looked you that way—you were with Tom. Plus he told me "I never really liked you that much; you were so controlling. We used to talk about Tom letting you control him like you did. You acted like you were always right about everything and better than everyone. Then guess what he said to me . . . it's really sad what happened to you in that accident. But you are actually a beautiful person now. I like you, he said. Boy was that nice to hear.

Another thing happened before this that was nice.

About a month before the Tony Bennett Concert, me, Chalie, Mary, Jerry, and a few friends went to an a cappella concert. Jerry was sitting next to me.

Before I took a sip from my wine I whispered to Jerry, "I want to say something to you before you think it's the drink talking. I'd like you to spend the night at my place tonight." "since it's only five blocs away, Chalie can drop us off. He seemed a little shocked and said okay. After Chalie dropped us off, Jerry said to me, that Chalie was really upset. Why, I asked. When I told Chalie I'm staying your place, he answered, "Jerry, do you know who that is? That's CarolAnn—what are you doing?" she asked me to come over so I am, he replied. Chalie just shook his head. Chalie knew me for a long time. Respected me, liked me and he never took advantage of me and didn't want Jerry to either. Plus Chalie knew I wasn't that kind of girl. I was so happy to hear that story. Respect is so nice and so important.

Charlie my good friend since "16" & Mary
with their daughter Jacqueline

So that night Jerry and I just talked and talked and laughed and had a good time together. We finally just fell asleep on the sofas. The next day, he went home. I really got to know Jerry that night—we never really talked alone for that long.

So life went on. I saw Jerry at Chalie and Mary's when I saw him. About three months went by and Jerry and I slept at Chalie and Mary's—no one wanted to drive me home—half an hour away. There wasn't room upstairs so Jerry and I slept on the floor in the living room. "and it just happened." It was so nonchalant—so comfortable and so nice. I fell more in love with Jerry that night and felt so much closer to him.

Jerry was so different than Tom. Didn't call much, didn't see him much. He lives an hour and a half away. He works 7 am to 3 pm. I work 3 pm to 9 pm. So it was hard talking and seeing one another. of course, not seeing him much made me want and miss him more. Plus when January came he went to Florida until April. He's a brick layer and it's too cold to work outside here

I wasn't used to seeing the man I loved so sparingly. So when I saw him I did complain of course. He'd say, "live like a gypsy—It's hard for me to have a girlfriend." Then he told me he's been single for 35 years and didn't have to call a girl to say what she was doing or where he was going. <u>And he likes it that way.</u> So we will just be friends. I tried to deal with that, which was hard for me. All my life, I was married and loved having my man around all the time.

So life went on with Jerry. Seeing him the most every two weeks—sometimes over night, sometimes one night. He always seemed when he woke up with me, he couldn't wait to leave. I knew he liked me but he couldn't handle me for too long. Not realizing I was a little too much at that time. Also, all I did was talk abut sex. I was still on my medicine—lithium to keep my blood level up to go to my brain where I lost my cells so new cells could grow back in time. And Zoloft, an antidepressant to keep me sane. Antidepressants are supposed to bring your sexual appetite to a lower level or to a close. But with me, it was the opposite. I wanted sex every minute. The doctor said, "you had a brain injury we don't know what happened up there; you're completely different." I used to call Jerry at least two-three times a week and talk about sex. Sometimes he'd like it, but when there were people in the room with him he didn't like it at all. Especially when he was in his mother's house. He would mad at me. He once said, "youre like a man with sex. You're a woman, act like one." He'd get so mad at me at times and he'd get so embarrassed when hi s mother was next to him. I was "out to lunch." I was also used to controlling Tom for twelve years—that's all I knew!

I learned so much from being with Jerry.

He is a man I look up to. He has his head so together—so popular—everyone loves him. He's so funny like "Jimmy Durante" even though he's not related to him ☺. He mainly taught me how to be "a woman." I feel more feminine than I ever felt in my life. I guess with my dad cheating on my mom and my mom never being happy, I wanted to control a man so I wouldn't get hurt. I came off so strong but was only a little girl inside.

Jerry used to yell at me at times when I got too demanding. He'd say, "you're not going to control me like you controlled Tom."

Jerry and I were seeing each other for eight years, which shocked him and me. Even though I didn't see him much—I loved when I was with him—even if it was only for hours. I'd rather have Jerry in my life some of the time than look for another man to be with me all of the time. I have so much fun with him.

He still makes me laugh. No man ever made me laugh after knowing them a few years. They'd get on my nerves a while. I always love being with Jerry—he's the first man I ever loved and also liked at the same time. And of course, I love sex with him more than everyone else. He still makes me melt when he touches me. Even when he just sits next to me! I love my sweetheart!

So before I end this book, Jerry and I were seeing each other for eight years when my doctor took me off my medicines. My blood pressures was going up higher, then high from lithium. I felt like I didn't need my antidepressant anymore. I was loving life. Content with myself. Living with myself for thirteen years alone now. Being more independent than I ever was. Not needing a man by my side to be happy in life. And not wanting to have sex every minute being on antidepressants. So I was of my medicine for two weeks—whining myself off them then taking an herbal pill, St. John's Wort 'cause I was crying over silly things (coming off my meds). So after about a month, I felt like Carolann DeBellis again for the first time since 1987. and of course, better. It's now 2002.

Jerry said to me soon after . . . "you were drugged for eight years. Since I've been with you." I asked, "how do you put up with me?" "I obviously care about you." I died and went to heaven again!

I don't call Jerry two-three times a week anymore. He calls me and he's more attentive! I'm not a sexual maniac anymore. I just want Jerry when he's next to me and sometimes when he's not. I see him more 'cause he likes being with me more now. And he tells me I'm invited to his home anytime I want to go. Go Bless. I'm more content than I've ever been in my life. When I miss Jerry, I go see him. He comes to my house when he can and we enjoy each other so much.

He told me once, "what I like about you the most is your independence." I love and like me—I love and like Jerry and I love and like life very much!

Thank you, Lord.

I love you so much!

Also, Thank God for Terri she was single at the time. We hung out together. Out to dinner and dancing..... having fun

Jerry & I as friends
New Year's Party 1989
. . . still married to Tom

Two years after seeing each other . . . going
on a cruise to Bahamas 1995

At the "Goo Q" . . . famous barbeque he
& his brother Steve (Goo) had for 25 yrs.
2000

Me & Jerry at Russo's Bar
2001

Exciting time bought my own car after
not being allowed to drive
for 4 yrs. Mom let me use hers for awhile
2002

I Love my Honda Civic

LIFE IS VERY SIMPLE . . .
YOU COULD LOVE SOMEONE VERY MUCH BUT IF YOU DONT LIKE THEM, EVEN DEEP DEEP DOWN, THERE'S SOMETHING MISSING. YOU NEVER LOOK UP TO THEM. LIKING THEM BRINGS IT ALL TOGETHER.

THE BOTTOM LINE IS . . .
YOU MUST LIKE YOURSELF FIRST.
IF YOU DON'T, YOU'LL ALWAYS LOOK FOR SOMEONE ELSE TO LOVE YOU—SO YOU'LL FEEL GOOD ABOUT YOURSELF.

LIKING AND LOVING YOURSELF FIRST IS VERY IMPORTANT.
. . . THEN YOU CAN GO ON IN LIFE DOING THE RIGHT THING.
THEN EVERYTHING WILL COME TOGETHER BEAUTIFULLY ☺
I WILL NEVER DIE IF I LOSE ANOTHER MAN IN MY LIFE.
BECAUSE I HAVE MYSELF.

THANK YOU, LORD.

I always loved reading and saving quotes.

**If I feel better about myself all of their talk won't bother me.
I can actually ignore!
. . . I could be a kind, considerate, fun-loving person
how much better I would feel.
. . . here are many that touched my heart. Many helped me
move on at difficult times of my life . . .**

Enjoy . . .

FORTITUDE

Dear JESUS, lay your Wounded Hand
Upon my weary head,
And teach me to have courage
In the paths that I must tread.
Bless me, and bless those
Whom I love,
And give us grace to see
These crosses bravely borne
By us
Will keep us close to Thee.
And if at times a shadow falls
In unexpected ways,
Please put Your gentle Hand in
Mine
And guide me through the days.
So bless my people, one and all,
With Thy protecting grace.
And impart to them Thy
Wisdom
Ere they meet Thee face to face.

We are healed of a suffering only be experiencing it to the fullest.

I believe . . .

If your dreams die, you die

If you don't stand for something, you'll fall for anything!

Don't forget "we are never perfect." You can always be better, we all learn everyday of our lives, from our experiences and problems and from other peoples' experiences and problems.

Love is the nicest gift of all.

Holding a cheerful attitude in mind and heart is an important part of living a happy, joy-filled life.

You're sitting on top of the world, then all of a sudden it comes crashing down.

When you love someone, it's the best.

However tough life gets, it's worth living.

In life, there is sadness and fear. And once in a while, a little happiness shows up.

All forgiveness is a gift to yourself.

Don't let anyone else you there are limitations. Don't let anyone tell you they can't do something. Find out if they can! Try!

The most precious gift is your heart.

When a person drowns himself in negative thinking, he is committing an unspeakable crime against himself.

Maxwell Maltz

Sit loosely in the saddle of life.

Robert Louis Stevenson

Be patient toward all that is unsolved in your heart/and try to love the questions themselves.

Rainer Maria Rilke

Life is not a "brief candle." It is a splendid torch that I want to make burn as brightly as possible before handing on to future generations.

George Bernard Shaw

Never let yourself use up today.

Richard H. Nelson

The important thing is to forget the past. Live for the present. If you can't forget the past, you stay in it and never get out.

He is a wise man who does not grieve for the things which he has not, but rejoices for those which he has.

And the day came when the desire to remain the same became more painful than the risk to evolve.

TIME & SPACE

There may come a time in your relationship when time and space are needed, to search your true feelings. It is a time to put your love to the test, even if it means making mistakes while doing this and this is what will happen if you don't. your partner may resent you for holding them back and push you further away. Don't make the same mistakes I made, because it will only make your partner resent you even more if you try to change the way they feel about things and it could start getting ugly for the both of you.

Don't let your emotions take over, use your head instead of your heart. If you don't, your emotions will make you do things, crazy things to drive your partner away and will destroy the love you have for each other.

Love is a funny thing, and nothing to play with. Don't push them too far, and do not question their actions by making them think that you are in control, because you're not, they are.

If you really love this person as much as you say, then let them go. I know for a fact that if you don't, you will lose the one you love forever and what you both had together will become a memory. Love, true love, only comes once in a lifetime and when it comes to you, you will know it.

Don't let the one you love get away, by not giving them the time and space they really need. Love is the strongest thing in the world, so don't let anything get in the way of love and remember, only love can break a heart.

"You have taught me how to love, but never told me that it would hurt"

1-14-91

You show your intelligence by your silence.

The Apostolate of Smiling
Just a little smile on your lips:
Cheers your heart
Keeps you in good humor
Preserves peace in your soul
Promotes your health
Beautifies your face
Induces kindly thoughts
Inspires kindly deeds

Your Smile . . .
Can be the beginning of conversion to the Faith.

Your Smile . . .
Can prepare the way for a sinner's return to God.

Your Smile . . .
Can win for you a host of devoted friends.

Smile, too, at God . . .
Smile at God in loving acceptance of whatever he sends into your life, and you will merit to have the radiantly smiling face of Christ gaze on you with special love throughout eternity.

Rev. Bruno Hagspiel, S.V.D.

First, learn to love yourself. Then you can love me.

When it gets the darkest, that's when the stars come out. We need to stay patient and let God take the controls.

Common sense is simply the instinct for doing the right thing at the right time.

I can learn to depend on myself. Maybe other people haven't been there for me but I can start being there for me. If I don't take care of myself, I wont be able to do much to help the people I love.

I can develop boundaries, limits that say, "this is as far as I'll go," and "this is what I won't tolerate."

It's okay to give to others, and it's okay to keep some for myself, too.

Today isn't yesterday. Things change. Just because it hasn't happened yet, doesn't mean it'll never happen.

I can learn to accept the darker side of myself. I can learn to accept the darker side of other people, too.

My source of happiness isn't inside other people. It's inside me.

Giving to people is an important part of living, but there's a big difference between giving and being robbed.

I have a right to be, to be here, and to be who I am.

My past has prepared me for this moment. Today prepares me for tomorrow. Nothing is wasted. Anything can happen, and "anything" doesn't necessarily mean something bad.

The problem isn't what other people have been doing to me. It's what I've been doing to myself.

I need to combine hard work with a lot of acceptance and letting go.

It's okay to be in a special love relationship. It's okay not to be in a relationship. It's okay to be looking for one.

I deserve the best love hast o offer. But the process of getting the best from love begins with me.

There's no such thing as a perfect person. There's no such thing as a perfect relationship.

Life is full of pain—the suffering is optional.

I can take all the time I need to collect my thoughts, resolve my feelings, and figure out solutions.

I don't have to give up my power to think, feel, and make good decisions to anyone or anything.

The only person I can change is myself. But, by changing myself, I may change more than I can imagine.

I cant change things I can't change, and trying to do that will make me crazy.

A relationship doesn't begin my life. A relationship doesn't become my life. A relationship is a continuation of my life.

I don't have to give up everything else for love.

Conflicts don't have to end relationships. Sometimes I need to work hard on a relationship. Sometimes I need to back off and work on myself.

Affirmations, positive messages, I choose to give myself, help create reality. Affirmations create space where reality can happy.

I don't have to be perfect, and neither does anybody else.

I don't have to be perfect. I don't even have to be nearly perfect.

I can learn to recognize when I'm reacting, when I'm allowing someone or something to yank my strings.

The best way to help other people is to keep doing my own work.

Having fun helps me stay healthy. It helps me work better. It balances my life.

Self-will usually doesn't work. Acceptance and letting go usually do work.

I can recognize the difference between relationships that work and relationships that don't work.

When I really trust that I'll take care of myself, I can let go enough to soar.

My first responsibility is to myself.

I can care about other people without letting them control me. My behavior never has to be "conditional" on another person's behavior.

I can't change who I am until I accept myself the way I am right now.

I can't change others, but I can change myself—one day at a time.

Sometimes we must set something free. If it returns, then and only then can it be ours.

If I'm not sure what I want, it's okay to wait. The answer will come. Decisions don't have to be made perfectly.

I can take responsibility for myself. I don't have to take responsibility for other people.

How I feel about myself makes a difference. What I tell myself makes a difference.

To let go and love other people, I need to feel safe and strong; I need to love myself.

I need love, but I don't need destructive love.

Life hold surprises. Lots of them are good.

If I want to change what happens, I need to change what I believe and expect.

If I'm willing to get honest, be open and try things differently, I'll change.

Feeling sad and angry is sometimes as important as feeling happy and peaceful.

Feelings aren't good or bad; they're just feelings. It's okay for me to have my feelings—all of them.

I don't need to take care of myself fin self-defeating ways. I can take care of myself fin positive ways.

I can trust my mind and my ability to think. I can take my brains with me wherever I go.

I can learn to be comfortable with myself and my life.

I can face my past and then leave it behind, if I choose.

I need to be gentle and compassionate with myself.

I have the right to change my own rules—the powerful messages from the past that control what I do today.

When I've done all I can do, it's time to let go.

I need to listen closely to myself to hear what I'm saying and thinking.

If I listen to myself, I'll probably hear myself say what the problem is. The next step is acceptance.

Barney says, "Most of the troubles in life are the result of saying a 'yes' too soon or 'no' too late."

We make a living by what we get, but we make a life by what we give."

St. Barnabas Church bulletin

We never get used to death because it's <u>always somebody different.</u>

God gives us as much as we can handle.

I know God won't give me anything I can't handle. I just wish he didn't trust me so much

Mother Teresa

The true measure of success in life isn't money, fame or power, it's laugh lines.

ONE DAY AT A TIME

We worry about tomorrows, often missing the joys of today, troubled about what may happen, yet tomorrow may not come.

Life's pathway is ever uncertain, right now is what's yours and mine. The future is safe in God's keeping. We can live but one day at a time.

St Barnabas Church bulletin

Control is an illusion. It doesn't work. I can't change other people.

If its yours it wont pass you by.

Laura Tomisetti

Life isn't always obedient.

Laura Tomisetti

A cup of tea is even more special when shared with a friend.

Sometimes, to find a solution, sit still and let it come to you.

The long view is ultimately the more accurate one.

It is good to know the truth but it's not always necessary to share it.

Barney says: A busy man may not be happier than an idle one. He just doesn't have time to notice it.

St. Barnabas Church bulletin

Forgiveness of one's enemies provides the ultimate victory.

The wise person does in the beginning what the fool does at the end.

When do you look for happiness? Some seek happiness by satisfying their every desire. <u>The more they get, the more they want.</u>

They become restless and frustrated in the pursuit of their elusive goals. Are you chasing after happiness? Do you believe you will be happy if you win the lottery, meet the right person, or get the right job? All these things are fleeting and are no guarantee of permanent happiness. <u>Happiness is impossible to find in material possessions.</u> Happiness comes not from trying to satisfy your wants as you <u>perceive</u> them, but a<u>ccepting life as it unfolds</u> and <u>trusting</u> that a loving God provides you with what you really need. Doing a good job, helping others, and including God in your daily life are keys to true and lasting inner peace and happiness.

Cardinal's Weekly Millennium Message

God's Will
I know not by what methods rare, but I know God answers prayer.
I know if the blessing sought will come in just the guise I thought, I leave my prayer to Him alone whose will is wiser than my own.

St. Barnabas Church bulletin

God's Design
Philosophers may reason why, but I won't take the time, I only know I'm here on earth because of God's design. So I will just continue on and do the best I can, and know that God will do the rest because He made the plan.

St. Barnabas Church bulletin

Your ability to relax is in direct proportion to your ability to trust life.

The way to win is to make it ok to lose.

Maturity consists of no longer being taken in by one's self.

Life always keeps its agreement with you.

He who laughs, lasts.

You are the only teacher you will ever have.

If you don't know what direction to take, you haven't acknowledged where you are.

A happy person is not a person in a certain set of circumstances, but rather a person with a certain set of attitudes.

Hugh Downs b. 1921
American Journalist

The more passions and desires one has, the more ways one has of being happy.

Charlotte-Catherine 17th
century Princess of Monaco

Blessed are they who can laugh at themselves for they shall never cease to be amused.

"A woman who will tell her age will tell anything . . ." that's definitely me ☺

Mary Kay

What lies behind us and what lies before us are small matters compared to what lies within us.

St. Barnabas Church bulletin

THINK
By Dr. Robert Anthony
You can only have two things in life, reasons or results. Reasons don't count.
If you are constantly being mistreated, you're cooperating with the treatment.
You don't have to be positive, you just have to be yourself.
You cannot control without being controlled.
They angry people are those who are most afraid.
There is no way to know before experiencing.
What you said is exactly what you intended to say.
The thing we run <u>from</u> is the thing we run <u>to</u>.
Consciously or unconsciously, you always get what you expect.
Others can stop you temporarily; <u>only you can do it permanently.</u>

Whatever you are trying to avoid won't go away until you confront it.

Most of our lives are about proving something, either to ourselves or to someone else.

If you don't start, it's certain you won't arrive.

What you can't communicate runs your life.

Your enemy might become your friend, if you allow him to be who he is.

If you worry about what might be, and wonder what might have been, you will ignore what is.

When you blame others, you give up your power to change.

Whatever you are willing to put up with, is exactly what you will have.

Your interpretation of what you see and hear is just that: your interpretation.

When you usually take a good look at your life, success is all you've ever had.

You are the cause of everything that happens to you. Be careful what you cause.

Feelings of inferiority and superiority are the same. They both come from fear.

What we are is God's gift to us. What we become is our gift to God.

Excuses are your lack of faith in your own power.

Things are not what they seem, they ar what they are.

If you are not leaning, no one will ever let you down.

God, give me the serenity to accept the things I cannot change, courage to change the things I can and wisdom always to tell the difference.

Man can have nothing but what he strives for.

I am not alone.

My dad . . . the first guy that ever loved me. The first guy I ever gave my heart to. ☺

I will never die if I lose another man in my life, because I have myself now. Thank you, Lord. Again.

God made me, no matter what I do.

If I am making a mistake, I need to make it.

We are all the embodiment of love. It is to know love that we are on this earth. That is what all the great beings have taught us.

I express the essence of who I am freely and lovingly.

I can have exactly what I want.

The weaknesses and sharing them is the power of our relationship.

I, Carol, lovingly release others to their own lessons.

It's ok to have needs and to ask for what I need.

I can trust myself.

Song in Spite of Myself
By Countee Cullen

Never love with all your heart
It only ends in aching;
And bit by bit to the smallest part
That organ will be breaking.

Never love with all your mind,
It only ends in fretting;
In musing on sweet joys behind,
Too poignant for forgetting.

Never love with all your soul
For such there is no ending,
Though a mind that frets may find control,
And a shattered heart find mending.

Give but a grain of the heart's rich see,
Confine some under cover,
And when love goes, bid him God-speed.
And find another lover.

Magee 2/12/87-3/26/87
First slip of paper Carol wrote
"When you love someone, it's the best."

Every sensation in life I enjoyed is mine for ever . . . I really didn't lose them.

I'd rather be celibate and lonely than have a man half-assed and be empty.

Happiness is like a butterfly: the more you chase the more it will elude you. But if you turn your attention to other things, it comes and softly sits on your shoulder.

Ten Rules for Success

1. find your own particular talent
2. be big
3. be honest
4. Live with enthusiasm
5. Don't let your possessions possess you
6. Don't worry about your problems
7. Look up to people when you can—look down to no one
8. Don't cling to the past
9. Assume your full share of responsibility in the world
10. Pray consistently and confidently

Do it now!

I shall pass this way but once, any good, therefore, that I can do or any kindness that I can show to any human being, <u>let me do it now</u>. Let me not deter or neglect it, for I shall not pass this way again."

Henry Drummon

Imagination is what keeps us pushing beyond what we believe our limits to be.

When in doubt . . . time out.

There's a Reason

For every pain we must bear,
For every burden, every care
There's a reason.
For every grief that bows the head,
For every teardrop that is shed,
There's a reason.
For every lonely pain-wrecked night,
There's a reason
If we trust in God as we should,
It will all work out for our good.
He knows the reason.

Life Center for Attitudinal Healing Principles

1. The essence of our being is love.
2. Health is inner peace. Healing is letting go of fear.
3. Forgiveness is the way to true health and happiness.
4. Since love is eternal, death need not be viewed as fearful.
5. We can let go of the past and of the future. Now is the only time there is.
6. We can become love finders rather than fault finders.
7. We can learn to love ourselves and others by forgiving ourselves and others rather than judging.
8. We are students and teachers to each other.
9. Giving and receiving are the same.
10. We can focus on the whole of life rather than the fragments.
11. We can perceive others or ourselves as either extending love or giving a call for help.

12. We can choose to direct ourselves to experience peace regardless of the events in our lives.

13. All minds can be joined.

14. Decisions can be made by listening to the preference for peace within us.

The principles of attitudinal healing are tools with which we can learn to make different choices.

Life Center for Attitudinal Healing
Guidelines for Center Activities and
Improving Communication Skills

1. Speak in the first person and from personal experience.
2. Listen to the speaker—send love an compassion.
3. One person at a time speaks, without interruption; no side conversations.
4. Ask for a moment of silence if you feel disturbed. This is to find your own inner peace.
5. We are friends and equals to each other. We don't give advice or counsel; however, we can share our first-person experience.
6. Confront no one. Avoid judging or arguing.
7. Confidentiality: Everything spoken in the group remains in the group.
8. Recognize that we do not have the power to change others, only the power to change ourselves.

The Life Center does not endorse any particular religious doctrine. We welcome all people and all religions.

Being innocent is not the same as being virtuous.

To be pitied is to be condemned for bad judgment or bad luck. Reputations aren't built on what one plans to do.

Intimacy and closeness requires self-acceptance. I need to be intimate with myself before I can be intimate with anyone else.

Sharing who I am and how I feel helps me get close to people.

Don't count the days . . . let the days count ☺

All of us are wounded in our family; it is important to make up for each other's imperfections. Only when we share forgiveness and understanding, will we experience the peace that Jesus promises today.

If you can't love yourself, how in the hell can you love someone else?

When you're giving, you don't have any experience. You're charged up and out of control. And if you're old and you're not charged up then all you have are memories. But if you're charged up and simulated by what's going on around you, and you also have experience, you know what to appreciate and what to pass by. And then you're really cruising.

Neil Young

There is a place within myself where I can go and always be relaxed and at peace and totally free to just be me.

There's no accidents . . . it happens at the perfect time.
My injury wasn't an accident. It was a miracle.

If I had my life to live over again,
I'd dare to make more mistakes next time. I'd relax. I would limber up. I would be sillier than I have been this trip. I would take fewer

things seriously. I would take more chances. I would take more trips, I would climb more mountains and swim more rivers. I would eat more ice cream and less beans. I would perhaps have more troubles, but I'd have fewer imaginary ones.

You see, I'm one of those people who live sensibly and sanely hour after hour, day after day. Oh, I've had my moments, and if I had to do it over again, I'd have more of them. In fact, I'd try to have nothing else. Just moments, one after another instead of living so many years ahead of each day. I've been one of those persons who never goes anywhere without a thermometer, a hot water bottle, a raincoat, and a parachute. If I had it to do it again, I would travel lighter than I have.

If I had my life to live over, I would start barefoot earlier in the spring and stay that way later in the fall. I would go to more dances. I would ride more merry-go-rounds. I would pick more daisies.

Nadine Stair

No one can make you feel inferior without your consent.

Eleanore Roosevelt

couldn't believe when she told me this story. She waited until I came home. I know I definitely saw him because I remembered the whole situation when she told me this story.

God does things in funny ways!

I know God helped me get through this. He made my grandmother and my Uncle Bill help me. I just wasn't ready to die yet. Got wants me to do more here!

This doesn't frighten me when I think about this. I think it's beautiful and this has brought me so much closer to God.

WE MUST HAVE FAITH!

. . . there is a reason for everything. You can't resent or say "Why did this happen to me." This made me a different person. And made me more aware of a lot of things in my life. It also changed a lot of my family members and friends.

. . . ALL FOR THE BEST.

. . . we're never perfect—you can always BE BETTER—WE ALL LEARN EVERYDAY OF OUR LIVES—FROM OUR EXPERIENCES AND FROM OTHER PEOPLE'S EXPERIENCES AND PROBLEMS.

Unfortunately, I lost my mother and father before my book got published.

Strange with both parents knew they were dying.

One good thing about that—you say things you probably wouldn't say if you didn't know they were dying.

My mom, who taught me right from wrong, died first. I always thought that she thought I loved my dad more than her. Because we got along better than she and I. So I said once, "I love you mom"—"I know," she said. "I thought you thought I loved daddy more." "no, I didn't," she said, "daddy never yelled at you telling you what to do—I did all that. That's why you think that."

Once she was looking at me real sad. I said, "what mom?" "I feel so bad that you're losing your mother." I can't believe she felt more bad for me and not herself. She had lung cancer, 74.

My dad, the first guy I ever gave my heart to, died only two years after Mom. He went from dementia to Alzheimers. He turned into a child—didn't know any of us for a while. But thank God, he came back ten days before he died and was daddy again.

I wrote the eulogies for my mom and dad and I'd like to share them with you.

Mommy's Eulogy
10-21-29 - 08-01-03

Anna Stella Pomante—Anne DeBellis—Aunt Annie—Mommy — Grandmom

. . . was a very, very independent and <u>strong woman.</u>

She was a wife and mother. Kept a beautiful home—was a great cook, which my father STILL talks about. She provided us with everything we needed while we were growing up. We always vacationed in Atlantic City for the summer. She loved the beach! She loved her Italian music. I remember her ironing for hours and singing with her music.

She was a hairdresser raising us. Then, she enjoyed working with children at Morton School.

"Annie loved her beer"

She was a hit at parties, singing her Italian songs and dancing while everyone joined in. She would do this with a small group of two to three people too. We are surely going to miss that Annie.

Her strength throughout her life made her strong in the end. The nurses couldn't believe how strong she was in her condition mentally and physically . . . helping move her own leg and arm as the nurse washed her everyday. NOT TALKING ANYMORE.

She would say what she really needed to. After being washed one day, nurse Tana said "bye Miss Anna, I love you." She answered, I love you too. The nurses loved my mom. They always told me how much she loved her children and didn't want us to worry. Mom loved her family and friends to visit, especially at the end. But loved her time alone too.

She would smile real big when we walked in.

One night, she looked at her night nurse, and said, "go home." "Miss Annie, I'm Judy, your nurse." "Go home now," she answered. The nurse called cousin Fred downstairs to make her feel safe. THANK GOD FOR FRED—he helped just being there in mom's last days.

Thanks, Fred.

My mom's biggest sadness she told me one day . . . was not seeing her grandchildren grow. After telling me she didn't want to die. "But we all have our time," she said. "Its now my time." SHE WAS SO STRONG, GOD BLESS HER.

My mom was pretty strict raising us. We'd get a look across the room. If we were doing or saying something wrong. I was still getting those looks sometimes.

My mother taught me right from wrong. Even through the difficult times in my life. I thank God for that. She made me the person I am today. And I like the person I am today.

Thank you, Mommy, we love you and will miss you very, very much.

We had a memorial for my dad and we just all stayed a few hours and talked about him.

Daddy's Eulogy
09-17-29 12-23-05

Rudolph Anacleto DeBellis (he changed Anacleto to James)
Rudy, Uncle Ru, Big Ru ('cause his son was called Little Rudy), Daddy, and of course, Grandpop.

My dad was an honest, happy-loving sensitive individual. He rarely got mad and he loved life! But when he did get mad, what a temper!

Unfortunately, I got that trait! Dad loved to talk and listen and help others with their problems. Therefore, he loved his profession as a hairdresser. Fortunately, I got those traits! Rudy was a famous hairdresser. He had the first wig shop in Philadelphia "The Wig Shop" 1718 Samson Street.

Dad did a wig for Diana Ross, Suzy Parker. And he cut Joe DiMaggio's hair every time he came to Philly to see family and friends. And he also cut Danny Thomas' hair once ;).

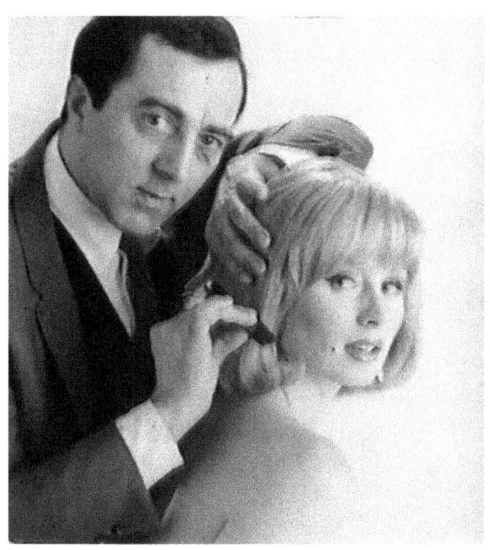

Daddy doing Suzy Parker's hair

Daddy w/ Joe DiMaggio's after cutting his hair

Daddy meeting Danny Thomas

Daddy loved his children more than anything in his life. He missed us when he went to work and he'd call in between haircuts when he could. When we were grown and on our own, we'd call . . . he'd get so excited when he'd hear our voices. Even if it was the day before.

Unfortunately, in his 60's, Dad was getting very forgetful and slowed down quite a bit. Dad had dementia and had to be put in Crest Haven nursing home two years ago. Thank God Crest Haven was a very nice home to be in. So clean and the staff really cared about their patients. They obviously liked their jobs. The staff always told us how much Dad loved us. He would always talk about us. And when he saw us, he would get so excited! I'd love walking into his room and seeing that.

Sometimes he'd ask "dad, why am I here with all these old people?'

I'd try to explain when we age, some things don't last. Bad heart, bad hip—legs, bad back, bad head.

Remember your dad's problem remembering. Couldn't go out alone. Afraid he'd get lost, etc. He did remember that! He knew he had a problem like his dad and was okay about being there. Thank God! Then, dad stopped remembering everything. Daddy now had Alzheimer's.

He didn't always know us. His eyes would look delighted for a second. Then he'd call me "miss" or just stare.

He stopped talking, stopped eating, stopped everything. So sad to see my dad like that! And so sad for his grandchildren to see. He got so bad in time and would just lay there and cry . . . saying help me help me!

What's wrong with me?

What a horrible disease. I'd pray for God to take him. I feel like my dad died six months ago. It wasn't him at all. My dad was so cool—inside and out! "cousin Fred" said he learned cool from Uncle Rudy. The doctors told us it was going to be soon. Dad had a very bad lung infection. We had to wear a mask, gloves, and a smock. Then, unbelievably so—dad came back to life. He was dad again. For ten days before he left us.

Every night. So glad I lived ten minutes away. He actually conversed with me. And ate all his food, which he hadn't done in six months. He'd say "thank you, Dad!" for what, dad? You are so good to me—you com every night and feed me. I said, Dad you were always good to me. I'm giving it back to you now. I'd then say "I love you dad" and kiss him through the mask he'd always answer, "I love you too, dad."

I could not believe he was talking again. He also kept looking up and talking. I couldn't understand a word. Just like my mom used to do when she was dying. Who are you talking to, dad? He never answered. Then, as I was giving him coffee, he'd say "Mommy makes the best coffee, don't she dad? Ask her to make more please!"

Then many times he'd ask . . . do you think Mommy would take me back? I love her soo much! I always loved Mommy! I know, Dad.

Then I kissed him; I love you, Dad. Love you too dad. The last night I saw my dad, he was looking up again and talking. I asked again, "who are you talking to, Dad?"

"My dad, I miss him and want to see him."

One nurse told me all week she caught him looking up and saying "I'm not ready yet!" I think he was getting ready now. I told him I wasn't coming the next night 'cause I was making ravioli with Jerry. He didn't answer me. He always said, "I'll be waiting" or "okay" when I'd say goodbye—I'll see you tomorrow. I couldn't leave that night, looking in the room. I kept going back. My dad left us at 7:00 the next night. He knew I wasn't coming. I'm glad I wasn't there. I'll miss seeing you daddy, but I know you're in peace and with your brothers-in-law, whom you asked for. And of course Mommy who forgave you before she died and many years before that.

Daddy, thank you for all that you have given me. And for all that you have taught me. I will miss you terribly!

I love you Dad . . . I know if you were here, you'd say back . . ."
I love you too, dad."

. . . MY MOTHER GAVE ME MY STRENGTH . . .

. . . MY FATHER GAVE ME MY DREAMS . . . Thanks mom and dad :)

Dad & Mom on their Wedding day 1952

I'd like to thank Michael and Meg again. If it weren't for them, this book could not have been written. Michael writing his journal while I was in my coma. I would not have known anything about that time. Of all his emotions, and how he helped me get through it all.

Meg, without you this book would have never been typed—I was writing and waiting for someone to come by that could type. I also needed to rewrite my book so it was legible, so I had to come to California to write it. Living my life, I never found the time.

I'd like to share with you one more thing before you close this book . . . when Meg brought me to meet my typist, I kept getting déjà vu's for twenty minutes meeting the girl sitting at the table with her grandchildren—being with an old friend I haven't seen in years. Pay bill, writing a book, booths in restaurant, granddaughter having to go to potty three times then my mother all around me. Then getting car, top of parking and grandson wanting to go all the way to the top— me calling Michael to talk about deja vu then telling him and Meg if it wasn't for you guys, this book would never have been written. Looking up at that same time I saw the letter "M" on the mountain (it was the Madonna mountain) reminding me again of God. Could it be? **Meg said her father also said when you have déjà vu's you are doing the right thing** ☺.

213

AUGUST 2012

I am now 59 years old. Living in Wildwood New Jersey.

Living on the water in a 2 bedroom apt. Every window I look out I see the bay. IT IS SO BEAUTIFUL! I LOVE where I live . . . . Even when I'm ALONE . . . . Jerry lives a few blocks away. We're together almost every day now. After 21 years. I have a great job cutting hair. Four days four hour days. I still love being a hairdresser after 34 years. AND I AM STILL helping people with their problems. I LOVE LIFE . . . Thank you Lord

BY THE WAY . . . unfortunately I got breast cancer 3yrs. In a row and had to retire. Cancer free for 4yrs :) All is fine. I'm still cutting hair for one's who need it.

Tom is also 59 now. Happily married, still living in Philadelphia. He and his wife Margaret are both realtors. I see Tom once and a while at funerals, etc. It is real nice sitting and talking with him. By the way. Tom is married to my cousin's ex wife.

I was almost over losing Tom when I found out he was seeing Margaret. So I didn't get TOO CRAZY maybe writing a letter or two to him and Margaret . . . .

Read between the lines.

THEY CALL ME TWO-TIME CAROL . . .

I always have something else to say . . . either calling back or walking back to the room or house where I was. :]

I found this in papers I had from years ago after my book was finally typed.

I guess this was supposed to be the last page of my book . . . It's funny when I look back and think about life and people . . .

There's so many of us that don't know ourselves. Everyone could say, "you're this—you're that—why don't you change." They answer, "Nothing is wrong with me-it must be you."

If my "Brain Injury" didn't happen, I would never have known I was so controlling in my relationships-in a friendship-and with my family.

I would never have gone to see a psychologist. I thought I was perfect and had no problems with myself.

Seeing a psychologist for four years made me see myself in a different light.

I wasn't happy unless I had a man to love me. A man I could control. So I could have everything I wanted . . . I would have never seen myself as that person.

Therefore, if anyone is not happy with their life or with the life they share with someone-go see a psychologist alone, or a marriage counselor with your mate. You learn so much about "you" that you did not see.

It's not that they tell you what you're doing wrong-you see it yourself. Because a psychologist is an outsider looking in, and could be so diplomatic.

You don't resent them or get mad. You just see light of your situation and yourself. :]

Seeing my psychologist doctor Brenda Ivker made me a better person than I ever was.

Knowing myself makes me deal with life SO WELL. It makes me understand life no matter how bad things can get . . . there is a reason and things can get better! And also, it will take you where you are suppose to be.

THANK YOU LORD FOR MY BRAIN INJURY!

LAST BUT NOT LEAST . . .

People ask me, How did you get over Tom?
. . . When I look back at it now . . .

It was the hardest thing I have ever had to go through in my life. It took me six years to actually get over losing my Best Friend and love of my life.

GOD HELPED ME THE MOST . . . I used to walk down the street just crying for no apparent reason at that time. I'd just look up and say . . . "I know this is happening for a reason God-I need to learn how to be with me-and to go on."

Another thing that happened intensely was looking at my Mother . . . still being so unhappy and bitter after losing my Dad in her fifties. Always feeling bitter about him cheating on her. She never went on. She never let another man in. Dad was ALWAYS there in her heart and in her head. She not realizing, it takes two to cheat and two to be unhappy.

Mom grew up with her dad cheating on her mother, so she constantly feared that and always accused him of cheating on her . . . so he finally DID.

Mom didn't forgive Dad until she was in her seventies. I didn't want to be like my mother in that way.

Plus another special feeling that helped me was . . . many people never in their lives ever find love-true love-special love-intense love.

. . . And I thanked God and still thank God that I had that love for twelve years.

. . . AND WE ALL KNOW . . .

"It is better to have loved and lost, then never have loved at all"

THANK YOU LORD, again!!!

www.ingramcontent.com/pod-product-compliance
Lightning Source LLC
Chambersburg PA
CBHW051303120626
46547CB00015B/2063